GOD'S JOYFUL PEOPLE —
One in the Spirit

GOD'S
JOYFUL
PEOPLE—
One in the Spirit

Oswald C. J. Hoffmann

Publishing House
St Louis London

Note. Quotations from Scripture are from a number of versions, including the King James Version, the Revised Standard Version, the New English Bible, Today's English Version, and J. B. Phillips' paraphrase, to bring out the force of the original.

Concordia Publishing House, St. Louis, Missouri
Concordia Publishing House Ltd., London, E. C. 1
Copyright © 1973 Concordia Publishing House

Library of Congress Catalog No. 72-96742
ISBN 0-570-03152-4

MANUFACTURED IN THE UNITED STATES OF AMERICA

Contents

Preface

Those who have heard the voice of Dr. Hoffmann on the International Lutheran Hour will hear his voice also in these pages. Bold, blunt, direct, and earthy, adjectives which characterize his weekly radio ministry, also characterize this volume. On every page there is the ring of assurance and authority.

And well there may be! For on every page Dr. Hoffmann, in words that are crystal clear, appeals to Holy Scripture as the final court and to Christ as "the Word of God Incarnate," God's all-sufficient and saving revelation to man.

In writing these ten chapters Dr. Hoffmann had a specific purpose in mind: to expound in lay language the Scriptural doctrine of the church. What *is* the church? Who started it? Who belongs to it? What kind of people make up its membership? What is the church's business? What holds it together? Where is it going? What about denominations?

Nor does he leave these questions hanging in the air. In each case he provides the clear-cut answer of the Scriptures. In a day of much confusion about the church, its mission and its ministry, Dr. Hoffmann has rendered an incalculable service by shedding Scriptural light on this important, timely subject.

Here is a book every Bible-believing church member, especially every layman who is looking for answers, will read with interest and with profit.

HERMAN W. GOCKEL

1. God's Colony

Colonialism has a bad odor these days. It smells of imperialism by which distant powers endeavor to impose their will and rule on weaker people struggling to get onto their feet politically, economically, and socially.

Eventually, if not now, history will probably record that the great 19th-century colonial powers which carved the world up among themselves performed some services for mankind along with all the grief they brought in terms of oppression and war. In some instances, at least, they helped to bring whole nations out of the stone age and, for good or ill, introduced them to the industrialism of the 20th century. At least some of the newly independent nations owe a great deal to the colonizers of Europe who, either consciously or unconsciously, helped them forge the tools by which they achieved national independence.

Nineteenth-century colonialism, which introduced so many peoples to the 20th century, had one fatal weakness. Like certain parents who do not like to see their sons grow out of knee pants, blind to the fact that their offspring have reached an age when they must begin to make their own decisions, so certain colonial powers of the 19th century closed their eyes to the fact that the 20th century had begun and that colonial peoples had to begin making their own decisions. In the violent upheavals that often resulted as colonial peoples asserted their independence, the good was frequently forgotten and the bad aspects of colonialism came to be emphasized to the exclusion of everything else.

North America would not be what it is today if it were not for those rugged people two centuries and more ago who braved the rigors of the wilderness and formed the 13 colonies which eventually became the United States of America.

It is an ironic fact that the most vocal and violent critics of colonialism in the modern world are themselves some of the most brutal and unscrupulous colonizers of all time. In almost every country of the world they have formed their own colonies of like-minded people, willing by subversion and treason to serve the best interests of their masters. All the while decrying 19th-century colonialism, they are building up their own form of 20th-century colonialism, promising all kinds of good for the world and actually delivering all manner of strife and conflict.

In this world of colonizers and colonials of whatever description, the great God has His own colony. It has a long history all its own, quite different from that of the world in which it is found.

God is not a politician. His colony does not have a political foundation or a political purpose. People of differing political convictions and economic views are perfectly content to live with each other in peace and harmony as members of God's colony. Knowing God, they trust Him and follow Him. While others are intent on declaring their independence of God, they find it all joy to belong to Him.

Who are these colonials of the Most High, carving

out a commonwealth for Him in the wilderness of the world? St. Peter describes them in the second chapter of his first epistle: "You are a chosen race, a royal priesthood, a holy nation, God's own people, that you may declare the wonderful deeds of Him who called you out of darkness into His marvelous light. Once you were no people, but now you are God's people; once you had not received mercy, but now you have received mercy." (1 Peter 2:9-10)

God's colony has a long and honorable history. In every age God has had a beachhead in the world — His colonial outpost pushing forward in the wilderness toward His promised land.

God's colony in the world came to public attention when a man named Abraham, obeying the Word of the Lord, moved from Mesopotamia to another land whose identity he did not know. The Lord God made a covenant with this man by which all the nations of the world would be blessed. Abraham would become the father of a special people, the bearers of this blessing, God's colony in the world.

At one of the most dismal points in their history the Lord God appeared to Moses with the reaffirmation of His covenant:

> I am the Lord. I appeared to Abraham, to Isaac, and to Jacob as God Almighty, but by My name, the Lord, I did not make Myself known to them. I also established My covenant with them, to give them the land of Canaan, the land in which they dwelt as sojourners. Moreover I have heard the groaning of the people of Israel, whom the Egyptians hold in bondage, and I have remembered My covenant. Say therefore to the people of

Israel, "I am the Lord, and I will bring you out from under the burdens of the Egyptians, and I will deliver you from their bondage, and I will redeem you for My people, and I will be your God; and you shall know that I am the Lord your God, who has brought you out from under the burdens of the Egyptians. I will bring you into the land which I swore to give to Abraham, to Isaac, and to Jacob; I will give it to you for a possession. I am the Lord." (Ex. 6:2-8)

Although God spoke thus to Moses, we are told the people did not listen because of their broken spirit and their cruel bondage.

God's colony had its ups and downs. Turning away from the Lord, as they did periodically, the people were recalled by the prophets to faith and service. The prophets kept reminding them that they were to be a beacon and a testimony to the rest of the world. Many took this mission seriously, looking upon themselves as true descendants of Abraham, strangers and pilgrims in the land, and looking forward to "the city which has foundations, whose builder and maker is God." (Heb. 11:10)

As their national fortunes declined, the people of God's colony maintained their hope in the great restoration to be effected by the One whom God Himself would send. It is interesting to read ancient Hebrew commentaries written before the time of Christ about the prophecies concerning the Messiah. Most of the passages looked upon by Christians today as foretelling the coming of Christ were similarly regarded by many of the ancient rabbis. They saw in Psalm 22 and Isaiah 53, for example, the picture not of a suffering nation but of a suffering Person, the Messiah promised long. Many such prophecies regarding the coming of Christ are to be found in the later books of the Old Testament. Finally, however, the voice of prophecy was stilled in the land. For several hundred years no books regarded as inspired by either Jew or Christian were added to the Scriptures.

Then it was, in the fullness of His own good time, that God sent forth His Son, made of a woman, made under the Law to redeem those that were under the Law. Christ was born, and a new age was ushered in — a new age better than the old one, and a new covenant to displace the old one.

The public life of the long-awaited Messiah was brief and stormy. After 30 years of obscurity He quickly rose to prominence. Three years He spoke in blunt, forceful, and outspoken language. Whatever else men may forget, they will never be able to forget Him.

Strange as it may seem, among His own kinsmen Christ's claim to be the long-awaited Messiah was looked upon as blasphemy and sacrilege. It did not occur to most of them that their rejection of Him and His subsequent execution put Him squarely at the center of the prophecy: "He is despised and rejected of men, a man of sorrows and acquainted with grief . . . . He was wounded for our transgressions, He was bruised for our iniquities; the chastisement of our peace was upon Him, and with His stripes we are healed." (Is. 53:3, 5)

People may forget, but the Lord does not forget His covenant. "You are a holy people to the Lord your God," Moses had said. "The Lord your God has chosen you to be a people for His own possession, out of all the peoples that are on the face of the earth. It was not because you were more in number than any other people that the Lord set His love upon you and chose you, for you were the fewest of all peoples; but it is because the Lord loves you and is keeping the oath which He swore to your fathers that the Lord has brought you out with a mighty hand and redeemed you from the house of bondage, from the hand of Pharoah, king of Egypt. Know therefore that the Lord your God is God, the faithful God who keeps His covenant and steadfast love with those who love Him and keep His commandments, to a thousand generations, and requites to their face those that hate Him, by destroying them; He will not be slack with him who hates Him, He will requite him to his face. You shall therefore be careful to do the commandments and the statutes and the ordinances which I command you this day."

With Christ the old covenant was done away and the new one began. With Christ there were to be no more ordinances, no more compulsory ceremonial observances, no more of the geographical and national lines forming the boundaries of God's colony. From now on people joined the colony right where they were. Now God would have His people in every nation to call on the name of the Lord and to be saved.

Disciples who had cowered behind locked doors for fear of what people might do to them stepped out into the open with the living Gospel: the Good News of Christ's death for the sins of the world and of His resurrection to be the living Lord of heaven and earth.

Receiving its orders, the colony of God moved out into the world. With firm voice and steady step its spokesmen stood up and talked up for God — conscious that they were God's own people, chosen by Him to declare the wonderful deeds of Him who had called them out of darkness into His marvelous light.

The story they told was quite simple. They described how Jesus of Nazareth was born, lived, suffered, and died. Having been with Him, they described what they had seen: "We saw His glory, the glory as of the Only-begotten of the Father, full of grace and truth." They spoke of His atoning death and of His victorious resurrection from the dead. They proclaimed forgiveness in His name, transmitting His promise of life and salvation to all who put their trust in Him. "Once you were no people," they said, "but now you are God's people; once you had not received mercy but now you have received mercy."

The Word of the Lord grew, and the colony took root in every land. Through the centuries it has had its ups and downs. When it looked as if the light might go out in the 18th century, there followed one of the greatest missionary forward movements in the whole history of the colony. Bearers of the Gospel, both pastors and laymen, went out into the world to carry out the mission of God's colony. Bible societies sprang up, and the Bible was translated into languages which had never known writing before. The Word of the Lord increased, and the colony took firmer root.

In the midst of the 20th century, with its nuclear power plants and its space vehicles, its solar batteries and pocket radios, its new clothing materials and its new medical cures, the colony of God gathered around the Word of God proclaims this fresh and vigorous message to the people of God: "You are a chosen race, a royal priesthood, a holy nation, God's own people, that you may declare the wonderful deeds of Him who called you out of darkness into His marvelous light. Once you were no people, but now you are God's people; once you had not received mercy, but now you have received mercy."

Refusing to be intimidated by persecution or power, the colony of God is still a foreign element wherever it is found. Its people are in the world but not of the world. They are not out to exploit people but to win them for God. Their purpose is not to perpetuate themselves but to bring glory to God. God's people are as busy and as constructive as a colony of bees.

If anyone wants to accuse God of being a colonialist, he can go right ahead. God is a colonialist. He has His colonies everywhere. Having established His beachheads in the modern world, He is not going to give them up. He has His men and women who have heard the call of their Savior: "If any man would come after Me, let him deny himself, take up his cross, and follow Me."

The colony of God is not an exclusive set of first-class snobs. It consists of people who have found forgiveness in Christ and who proclaim forgiveness to all men as Christ would have them do.

Christ is for everyone. He invites all people into the fellowship of faith—that family in which He is Brother and God is Father. By faith in Christ we join God's family, God's own people, God's colony in the world—chosen, set apart, and (because it has a divine Savior who forgives sins), by His own divine gift, holy!

2. The Church: Shepherd and Sheep

"I am the Good Shepherd," said Jesus Christ. He did not have to draw a picture for the people of His time. They knew what He was talking about. They saw it every day in the fields, on country roads, and even on city streets. In that part of the world, in central Europe, in the highlands of Colorado, on the coasts of Australia you can see it today. You don't have to go back to ancient times to get the picture.

Jesus Christ was not explaining shepherds; He was explaining Himself:

> I am the Good Shepherd. The Good Shepherd is willing to die for the sheep. The hired man, who is not a shepherd and does not own the sheep, leaves them and runs away when he sees the wolf coming; so the wolf snatches the sheep and scatters them. The hired man runs away because he is only a hired man and does not care for the sheep. I am the Good Shepherd. As the Father knows Me and I know the Father, in the same way I know My sheep and they know Me. And I am willing to die for them. There are other sheep that belong to Me that are not in this sheepfold. I must bring them too; they will listen to My voice and they will become one flock and one Shepherd. (John 10: 11-16)

The oneness of the whole arrangement is the impressive thing. In a world torn apart by its hatreds and hostilities, its envy and its selfishness, there is this Shepherd and there is His flock. The two belong together. You can't separate them. There is the Shepherd and His flock, there is Christ and His church.

That is the one thing a lot of people forget. Enemies of the church down through the ages just wouldn't believe it. Their bones lie rotting in the sands of time, but the church lives. A lot of people inside the church act as if it isn't true. You would almost think that the whole thing depends on them. If it weren't for them, the church would die. If you don't listen to them, you haven't got a leg to stand on.

There is only One who could talk big like that. "My sheep will listen to My voice," He said, "and there will be one flock and one Shepherd."

People don't like to be compared to sheep. Sheep are so likeable, but they can also be so dumb, so erratic, so helpless without leadership. They do such stupid things when just a little brainwork would keep them out of trouble. They cut off their noses, so to speak, to spite their faces. It is ironic, isn't it, that human history is largely a story of people defeating the causes they thought they were advancing.

The comparison goes back a long way. "All we like sheep have gone astray," said the prophet; "we have turned every one to his own way." The diagnosis is simple, direct, swift, and devastating. That's the way it is. A woman with everything to live for throws it away on frivolity. That huge success in business proceeds to make a mess of his life with a brainless performance that is utterly unbelievable. A boy with his whole future before him won't listen to anybody. He has got to have his own way, even if it means wrecking his life. Girls do the same thing. It's the human way: "All we like sheep have gone astray, we have turned every one to his own way."

We are told by St. Matthew that Jesus looked upon the mass of humanity and felt compassion. They were as sheep milling about, He said, without a shepherd. "I am the Good Shepherd," He said. "The Good Shepherd is willing to die for the sheep."

There are plenty of hired men around, but only one Shepherd. The Shepherd is willing to die for the sheep. The hired men are willing to lead, up to a point, but the Shepherd bleeds. He bleeds for the sheep.

Jesus Christ did not treat lightly the waywardness of man. He did not pass off the problem of humanity as we often do, half gaily and half wistfully, when we say: "To err is human." Of course, it is human. But that's not the end of it. Jesus Christ, the Son of God, came into the world to live and to die as proof of the desperate situation of man, tangled in his sin, his mistakes, his malice. Jesus Christ could not afford the luxury of a maudlin sentimentality which assumes that the situation of man is not as bad as the preachers make it out to be. Jesus Christ said man is not what he was meant to be. He isn't and, on his own, he won't be. The situation will not get better; it will only get worse. People are like sheep. They are lost. They can't find their own way. "I am the Good Shepherd," He said. "The Good Shepherd is willing to die for the sheep."

Sacrifice is at the heart of salvation. Parents sacrifice; they give up things for their children, and that's great. They do it because they love. Nothing else could make them do it. Sometimes fathers and mothers complain that their sacrifices have been met only with ingratitude. Probably they shouldn't complain, because the sacrifice may not have been as selfless as it appeared to be on the surface. Parents wanted to enjoy some of the results themselves.

Gaining the lost ones is not easy. It takes love of a high order. Love without thought of return—that's the love of Christ. It makes Him unique. He is the one Shepherd our world needs. Without Him, I am persuaded, the lostness of our world cannot be overcome.

The love of Christ, said one of His men, is simply beyond belief. It passes knowledge. Jesus Christ was aware of that. What He felt inside reminded Him of His Father: "The Father loves Me because I am willing to give up My life in order that I may receive it back again. No one takes My life away from Me. I give it up of My own free will. I have the right to give it, and I have the right to take it back."

The Shepherd pleads, and the Shepherd leads. That's Jesus Christ, Son of God and Savior of the world.

Jesus Christ died. That's a fact. Jesus Christ died for the sins of the world. That's the faith of the church. Throughout our world there are people who have faith in Christ that He died for all, including them. This is faith, when a man says, "Jesus Christ died for all and He died for me." Anybody can see that, and it is true. You can say it right now, and right now it will be true for you. You don't have to know everything about Christ to say it. You know He died for all, and that includes you.

Right now all you have to do is to turn from that way of yours and say to Him, "I believe You. You died for me. I go with You." You can say it to Him directly, for He is alive. Christ gave His life willingly; He sacrificed Himself out of pure love. He did what His Father commanded Him to do. "The Father loves Me," He said, "because I am willing to give up My life in order that I may receive it back again." He died for you, and He received His life back again. He was raised from the dead by the glory of His Father. He lives. He is alive. He is Lord, and He commands your faith. Don't be afraid to say it to Him: "I believe You." In that faith there is forgiveness for the past and life for the future.

Nothing but faith will do, faith in Christ the living Lord. It isn't easy, I know. It wasn't easy then. People gathered around Him and said, "How long are you going to keep us in suspense? Tell us the plain truth: Are You the Messiah?" Jesus answered: "I have already told you, but you would not believe Me. The works I do by My Father's authority speak on My behalf; but you will not believe because you are not My sheep. My sheep listen to My voice; I know them, and they know Me. I give them eternal life, and they shall never die; and no one can snatch them away from Me. What My Father has given Me is greater than all, and no one can snatch them away from the Father's care. The Father and I are one."

Jesus Christ did not go around telling people that

22

He was a good man. He said, "I am the Good Shepherd." A good shepherd is willing to die for the sheep. He did not go around proclaiming how great He was. He didn't have to. The greatness was there in everything He was and everything He did. "The works I do by My Father's authority speak on My behalf." That's a simple statement of fact.

Looking at the people in front of Him, all of them of one nationality, one country, one family, Christ said, "There are other sheep that belong to Me that are not in this sheepfold. I must bring them, too. They will listen to My voice, and there will be one flock and one Shepherd." That's the way it is. There is one body, and He is the Head. There is one flock, and He is the Shepherd. You can't split up Christ and His Father, and you can't split up Christ and His church. It's all one, one in Him.

There are all kinds of people in this church of His, all kinds of sheep in this flock of His. Some bear scars, and some don't. Some have had a rough time, and some have known peace all their lives. Some have had a great experience of faith, arriving at their convictions in a dramatic way. Others with faith just as deep never had such an experience. It isn't the experience that saves, but faith in Jesus Christ. "My sheep listen to My voice; I know them, and they follow Me. I give them eternal life, and they shall never die; and no one can snatch them away from Me."

There are all kinds of folds in this flock of His. I have never met one congregation of Christian people that looked exactly like another one. Each one is made up of people, and they are all different. It is an illusion to think that the church of Jesus Christ is going to look the same all over the world. It doesn't, and it won't. The church is an army of the living God, made up of a lot of regiments, each with a character all its own.

There is really only one flock and only one Shepherd. There are many folds, but one flock. Wherever Christ is Head, there is His church. If there is only one person who believes in Christ, there is His church. He knows that one; that one hears His voice and follows Him. That's the church.

Sheep flock together to follow the shepherd. There are some people around who are called "pastors," which means shepherds. They are not hired men; they speak for Him. They want people to hear His voice and follow Him — not to follow them but to follow Him. You can always tell the difference between a true shepherd and a hired man. A hired man thinks of himself, but the shepherd thinks of the sheep. A real pastor hears the voice of Christ and follows Him in exactly the same way as the people whom he serves follow Jesus. They do this because they hear His voice, the voice of the Good Shepherd.

The Shepherd bleeds for the sheep, and the Shepherd leads the sheep. The Shepherd pleads for His sheep. If any man sins, we have Someone who pleads for us with the Father, Jesus Christ the Righteous One. He leads in the paths of righteousness. He knows the sin of humanity, and He forgives. He knows the perplexity of humanity, and He leads through it all. For His name's sake He leads. "I am the Good Shepherd," He says. That's His name. "The Good Shepherd is willing to die for the sheep."

Christ's people know Him. They hear His voice and follow Him. Know Him, my friend! Listen to His voice and follow Him! It's your way out, the way of salvation for you. Go His way. It is a good way.

3. The Church Newborn

Christ's people are those ordinary folk who have found Christ. You find them all over the world today, with all the pressures of modern life upon them. If Christ's people needed reminding in the apostolic age, followers of Christ today probably need to be reminded too. "Through the living and eternal Word of God you have been born again as the children of a Parent who is more than mortal," said the apostle (1 Peter 1:23). This is God the Father.

People outside the church wonder what it is like to be on the inside. This is it: It is like being born again, getting a new lease on life, acquiring a whole new attitude, developing a new personality — and the whole thing comes from God the Father Himself. That's what it's like, that's what it is.

All of it began with God. You know what it cost, said St. Peter, to set you free from the worthless manner of life you received from your ancestors. It was not something that loses its value, such as silver or gold; you were set free by the costly sacrifice of Christ, who was like a lamb without defect or spot. Through Him you believe in God, who raised Him from death and gave Him glory; so your faith and hope are fixed on God.

Something happens when people get to know Christ, really to know Him. It is not mere repetition of some half-understood slogans, the kind of thing with which many people who call themselves Christians seem to be very well satisfied. I have to say this, because that kind of halfhearted Christianity never encouraged anyone to learn to know Christ and to follow Him. There isn't any force in it, and people outside the church see that right away. Often they see it better than people inside the church. So many in the church are satisfied with a mere profession that never has any practical results in the lives of people.

When people get to know Christ, something happens. "Knowing Christ," said St. Peter, "you purify yourselves by obeying the truth, and have a sincere love for your fellow believers; you love one another earnestly with all your heart. For through the living and eternal Word of God you have been born again of a Parent who is immortal, not mortal."

What the world needs today is a church that is newborn. The world has had its fill of churches that try to satisfy the hunger of people with theological piffle and sociological jargon. The world is completely turned off by churches that argue among themselves about the height of the cemetery fence while the world is careening toward hell. New buildings and bigger budgets, liturgical splendor and sensational innovation, useful as they may be, do not hold within themselves the answer to the world's problem. The apparatus of the church is just a means to an end. Of what value is it if the church has no end, no aim, no goal, no purpose that consumes its energies with passion for genuine accomplishment? What good is the church if it just idles along, as the world idles along, with little to go on and nowhere to go?

Wherever the church is the church, the body of Jesus Christ, it has a great thing to go on and a great way to go. There is no substitute for going. As Christ's men saw it, the church is alive, reborn, given new life, something that people never had before until they came to know Jesus Christ and to go with Him.

These men know what they are talking about. They had experienced it themselves. They saw what it was like before and after. Before they came to know Christ they were pawns, victims, playthings of the disintegrating forces of the world, of the fragmented purpose of the world, of the disenchantment of the world. After they came to know Christ they had purpose and vision, a good reason for tackling the difficult, the intricate, and the impossible. Their lives had been a cycle of blasted hopes and disillusionment, of trial and error, of random commitment and random decommitment. When they found Christ, they became part of something. Indeed, they became part of Someone. They were born again by the eternal Word of God. All of a sudden they knew themselves to be the sons of God. He was their Parent, not mortal as all of us parents are mortal, but immortal as only God can be.

They knew for sure that Jesus Christ died for the sins of the world, offering a costly sacrifice to redeem people from the worthless manner of life received from their forefathers. This Christ was raised from the dead, risen and victorious, and now He reigns over all things. They knew Him, and when they found Him they found themselves.

Like in Christ is a great thing. It has got joy in it,

a new way of looking at things, a new way of doing things, a new way of thinking, and a new way of acting. Life in Christ is a constant and open challenge, bright and rich with possibilities, but at the same time it is secure, rooted in a victorious, reigning, and everlasting Lord. His life becomes the life of all those who follow Him.

Christians are people who have tasted the goodness of the Lord. They are that if they are Christ's men and women, Christ's boys and girls.

This is God's design. He made it that way. The church is not just another social institution like the other institutions of the world. Those institutions come and go. They have life for a short time, and then they die. It is true of all of them. But the church lives on. You might say that it lives on in spite of the people who belong to the church. It lives on because it is the body of Jesus Christ, the suffering Son of God, raised to a position of power and glory by the design of His Father.

The church lives by the Word of God. Peter stated, "The Scripture says, 'All men are like grass, and all their glory is like its flowers; the grass dies, and its flower falls off, but the Word of the Lord remains forever.'" "This is the Word," he added, "that the Good News brought to you."

The Word of God lasts. It doesn't die out. It is an abiding, a living Word. It is a remarkable Word, coming alive in a living person, Jesus Christ.

In times past God talked to men at different times and in various ways through His prophets. Some were historians, others were poets; some were statesmen, others were farmers. God spoke through them to His people, stirring up a new kind of life to replace the old, worn-out ways that are characteristic of our world. But now He has spoken to the world in His Son Jesus Christ. That's where the life is, in Christ. In Him is life, and His life is the light of men. He died for sin, and sin is forgiven. He laid His life on the line, and in Him there is life for all. He cuts through all the moral chaos, the mess in the world. The obedience of faith in Him brings life and liberty, freedom to be His people and to do as His people. It is like being born again. It *is* being born again. "Through the living and eternal Word of God you have been born again as the children of a Parent who is immortal, not mortal."

The purpose of Christ's church in the world, the goal toward which it drives, is resurrection. It is like the resurrection of Christ Himself. It is coming alive after being dead. It is like being raised to life again, a new beginning, a new birth, a new everything. All of it happens through the Word of God, the Good News of Jesus Christ, of the smiling face of God, of the grace of God, of the goodness of God, offering forgiveness to a world that does not like to talk about its rebellion against Him and does not particularly want to be forgiven.

People today crave something that will get them out of the mess they are in. I have noticed they will try almost anything, from desperate schemes of self-help to the most outlandish religious superstition and supernaturalism. Self-improvement won't do it, and mere religion won't do it either. Only the good Word of God, the lively and life-giving Good News of Jesus Christ, ever produces real change, real life, real hope, real joy, and real courage. That's what the Word of God does, the Word of the Lord that remains forever, the Word that the Good News of Christ brings to people even today.

Where do you find the Word of God acting that way? I find it among people who do the Word of God. They are doers of the Word and not hearers only. It is something like the Lord Himself, who said, "My business is to do the will of Him who sent Me." In doing the will of His Father, Jesus Christ found strength and renewed resource for going ahead, for living, and even for dying with confidence in His Father. The Word of God produces faith, faith produces love, and love produces a lot of things. That kind of stuff belongs to people who use their spiritual muscles and don't allow them to return to flab. They believe in God, and they act for God. They don't run scared, because they don't have to. They go forward with courage, with a light in their eyes, with intelligent minds and warm hearts that come from God Himself.

There is nothing inactive or self-centered about people who are born again by the Word of God. They have tuned in on God, and you can hear the sound whenever they open their mouth. They have seen God, and you can see the light of it in their eyes. They crave, as others do, but they crave the Word of God as children crave milk to stay alive.

The Word of God, the Good News of Jesus Christ, is the life of the church. It always has been and it always will be. That is why the Scriptures are so important in the life of the church. They are not a club with which to beat other people over the head.

They are the life-giving power of God, bringing good news to a world which needs the salvation of God very much. Unless God saves, nobody will. If He can't be trusted, nobody can. If he doesn't exist, we are really in a mess. But the Word of the Lord remains forever—the Good News bringing salvation to all men everywhere. Crave it, have it, live it. It's the way to salvation, to life in all its abundance. "Through the living and eternal Word of God be free again as children of a Parent who is immortal, not mortal."

If you wonder what is wrong with the church today, this is it: So many people in the church are apathetic to the Word of God. They are neutral, half-believing and half-unbelieving, half-faithful and half-unfaithful, half-loving and half-unloving, half-ready to hear the Good News of Christ and half-unready, half-interested in other people and half-uninterested. There isn't any life in that kind of stuff.

When the early Christians were baptized, it was like getting a new life, like entering a new world. Christ was born in them. With them the whole church was reborn. It was like Easter morning, when Christ rose from the grave. Christ was raised from the dead by the glory of His Father, said St. Paul, and that's the way we walk in newness of life.

The Word of God takes hold of the ills of life, and it cures them. The Word of God takes hold of the ills in your life, and it cures them. It grabs all the guilt and buries it. That is what the death and burial of Jesus Christ means for you. Christ is the death of sin. Forgiveness puts it out of the way, and His resurrection opens a new door leading to a new life, all through faith in Him. Faith in Christ works. It works new life and produces new attitudes. It makes for new action with love, genuine and unbeatable love, taking the place of hostility.

Where do you find that today? I find it in the church, the church newborn. I must admit that not every member of the church is the best example of the new life in Jesus Christ. Some don't have that new life at all, and some are just learning it. Some haven't grown up very much, and some are stunted in their growth. Others are simply great. They don't care about power or prestige. They don't worry about popularity or unpopularity. They just love the Lord Jesus Christ, and they have life. They shine like lights in the world. They are good fathers and mothers, and their children respect them because they know what they are. They are good neighbors, and the community can always depend on them to do what is right, even if it hurts.

Our world needs people like that. They aren't just pious; they believe. They don't just say nice things, but they act in ways that are helpful to others. They have a mind for God and a heart for their fellowmen. They are God's children, newborn through the living and eternal Word of God which remains forever. It is Good News, and it brings new life.

The Word of God is the key. For everyone who craves salvation, rescue from the sordidness of life, here is the key. He need only take it and open the door. The Word of God is the Good News of Christ. He died for all, and He lives for all. Christ died and rose again from the dead. That's the sensational Good News. The Word of God offers us faith to believe it. What I am writing about right now is the Word of God. We are urged to take it and open the door to a new beginning, a new life, new hope, new joy, new courage. They're ours for the taking.

4. On Being the Church

What does it take to have a church? Some people are ready to answer that one right off the top of their heads. It takes a building, preferably of stone or brick — although a nice white frame structure in the old style looks mighty pretty, especially on a grassy slope overlooking a field or a lake. You have got to have a place where something called "services" are held. Then you have got a church.

Others think of a church as a kind of organization, a sort of club with executives and secretaries, presided over by a member of the clergy. Belonging to the club are some well-behaved citizens, well-dressed, fairly well educated, pretty well housed, some of them earning good pay and all of them well-intentioned. Some of the members of the club, apparently, think the purpose of the organization is to provide a forum or an arena where they can say and do anything that will thwart the pastor of the church, whom they consider to be a fuddy-duddy and wish that he would accept a call to some other congregation where he might feel more comfortable. Still others spend their time browbeating the clergyman, branding him a liberal because he has told them something or acted in a manner they had not known before.

There are good people in the community who think of the church as a stabilizing influence, vaguely and mysteriously shooting good impulses up the streets and down the avenues. The church is a stabilizing influence, they say, if it keeps the community from changing and prevents the crime rates from shooting out of sight.

For large numbers of people the church is just the source of a never-ending flow of letters, postcards, posters, bulletins, magazines, tracts, flyers, reports, envelopes, statements, phone calls, and announcements of sauerkraut suppers, strawberry festivals, ladies' bazaars, and just ordinary meetings. If these things keep coming, they feel the church is still active.

Such popular conceptions of the church, often held by church members themselves who think of the church in exactly the same way, cause people in almost every part of the world to look upon the church as the vestigial remains of a bygone age, an anachronism at the end of the 20th century, an institution that is dying but is too stupid to see what is happening, the spiritual equivalent of the steam engine or the horse and buggy.

There is good reason for talking today about what it takes to be a church—or better still, what it takes to be *the* church. It takes a lot, as St. Paul told one of the young churches of the apostolic age—a church, by the way, that needed a good dose of the potent vitality our churches need today if they are to be the church.

To his Christian readers St. Paul made it perfectly clear that, wherever the church is the church, the usual distinctions go by the board. In the church there are no Gentiles and Jews, circumcised and uncircumcised, barbarians, savages, slaves or free men, but Christ is all and Christ is in all.

Wherever the church is the church, Christ is everything. He counts, more than anything else or anyone else. What He has done—His death on a cross, His resurrection from a grave—has brought the church into being. What He has done and even now does as the living Lord of heaven and earth keeps the church going. Without Him the whole thing goes to pieces. If only one man were left in the church, He would be the one. The church is His body, and nobody is going to put Him out of the way or even put Him in the shade.

If this is true, that Christ *is* the church and the guarantee of its existence, that Christ is the core of the church's being, that the presence of Christ is the test of its very life, all of us had better look at the church again to see what it is all about; we had better look at what the church is doing in the light of what it *must be* if it is to be the church.

What does it take to be the church? St. Paul answered that question when, for example, he wrote to the people at Colossae, who were followers of Christ:

> You are the people of God; He loved you and chose you for His own. Therefore you must put on compassion, kindness, humility, gentleness, and patience. Be helpful to one another, and forgive one another, whenever any of you has a complaint against someone else. You must forgive each other in the same way that the Lord has forgiven you. And to all these add love, which binds all things together in perfect unity. The peace that Christ

gives is to be the judge in your hearts; for to this peace God has called you together in one body. And be thankful. Christ's message, in all its richness, must live in your hearts. (Col. 3:12-16)

Wherever the church is really the church, everything it is and everything it does begins with God. In the Old Testament God and His prophets say to His people, "You didn't choose Me. I chose you." He said that to keep them from getting to be proud and arrogant, from thinking that they could talk and act in any way they pleased and it wouldn't make any difference. Jesus said to His disciples, "You did not choose Me, but I chose you." That's the way Christ does things. That's the way God does things. He acts first, and He comes first.

The Christian church did not get started because a few fellows sitting around a table one night decided it would be nice if they had a place they could get together once a week. The church, wherever it is the church, is Christ's doing, God's doing. "You are the people of God; He loved you and chose you for His own."

It is a remarkable fact that God is still at it, gathering sons and daughters around His family board even in a world like our own — in a secular age where it has become somewhat fashionable to act as if you can get along very well without God. But God is still at it, with a kind of adoption procedure that brings people in who did not count themselves as sons and daughters of God until they came to know His own great Son, Jesus Christ. When they came to know Him, everything changed. In Christ they found God reconciling the world to Himself and not counting their sins against them. It is great good news that God feels this way and that He acts this way even today. It grips a man to know that Christ died for him, and it melts a woman to hear that Christ rose from the dead with God's own guarantee that forgiveness is not merely a possibility, or even a probability, but an actuality. Christ lives and Christ rules. He is worth trusting; He is worth following.

None of us did anything. God did everything. He gave His only Son. He gave Him for you. He calls you to be His son or His daughter by faith in Jesus Christ. He is even now drawing you into the circle of His family. Come in and sit down! You belong to Him because His Son laid down His life for you. Belonging to God in Christ, you are one of the people of God; He loves you, and He chose you for His own.

It's an honor to be a member of His family, to belong to the people of God. A lot of people are so conscious of the honor that they forget what it means. They put a little halo around their heads and go around challenging other people to knock it off. They act as though Christ did not die for everybody in this wide world of ours. You think that God had picked them out because they were so good, when the real reason is that *He* is so good. He invites everyone. If you belong, it is because He loved you and chose you for His own. You are the people of *God,* said the apostle to the church. Now act the part!

What does it take to be the church? It takes people who know what this means: "You are the people of God; He loved you and chose you for His own."

What does that mean, anyway? It means that you

can't go on acting, St. Paul said, like a club of first-class snobs who think they are better than other people. You can't ignore the world around you as if it does not exist. You can't pretend that there are flies on the other guys, but not on you. "You are the people of God; He loved you and chose you for His own. *Therefore* you must put on compassion, kindness, humility, gentleness, and patience. Be helpful to one another, and forgive one another, whenever any of you has a complaint against someone else. You must forgive each other in the same way that the Lord has forgiven you. And to all these add love, which binds all things together in perfect unity."

The criticism of the church has been coming thick and fast from all sides. Some of this criticism is unjustified. It is clearly the result of misunderstanding, which is all too common in our world. The early Christians were accused of being cannibals by people who did not understand what happened at the Lord's Supper, where Christians receive the body and blood of our Lord as His own gift in the bread and the wine which they eat and drink at this sacred meal.

When I was in the Far East some time ago, I found that Christians in a certain country are being criticized by their fellow citizens because they don't cry at funerals of their loved ones. Now, this is a misunderstanding. Christians cry all right, but not as those who have no hope. They hope in Christ for a great unveiling of life still to come, and that changes everything — even the deep feeling of loss they experience over the death of someone who is near and dear to them.

Some of the criticisms of the church are justified. Christians do not always live up to their fine professions. Some of them don't even try. Indeed, there are some Christians who know how to say all the right things but never even try to do things right.

The church has always been far from perfect. There is no excuse for inaction or for action that is downright wrong. Yet you will find both in the church. Even in the days of the apostles there were factions and fights, divisions and dissensions. There was condemnation then from people inside and outside the church, as there is a lot of criticism of the church today for the same reason.

There are hypocrites in the church, people who have no intention of living up to their calling as Christ's followers. There are Christians who are disinterested, uncommitted, or unwilling to accept the full responsibility of being a member of God's family. But then there are also Christians, a lot of them, who want to do the right thing and don't always succeed. Undoubtedly we are among them. We are always on the way, but the ultimate goal always somehow seems to elude us. We are like sons and daughters who have to be told and reminded every now and then of what it takes to be a responsible member of the family.

What does it take to be a responsible member of the body of Christ, so that the church may be the church? "Put on compassion, kindness, humility, gentleness, and patience," said St. Paul.

These are not common qualities in our world, despite all the talk in newspaper columns about the raising of children or about the crucial human rela-

41

tionships that have gone to pot in the morass of hatred and hostility, of selfishness and self-seeking, of impurity and immorality that have made our world what it is.

This is what it takes in our kind of world to be the church according to St. Paul:

Put on a new suit of clothes, put on your new dress. Dress yourself with compassion, with the ability and the readiness to care when other people are saying, "I don't have time . . . I can't be bothered . . . I have got my own problems."

Put on kindness and refuse to be overcome by sarcasm, bitterness, and nitpicking.

Put on humility, a mighty unpopular garment, in the place of the more popular ones: pride, boastfulness, and self-pity.

Put on gentleness, that quality of true gentlemen and real women who have minds of their own but don't try to dominate the lives of others, who don't have to run the show in order to play the game.

Don't forget patience. It understands how slow change can be, how much education it takes to produce action, and how others, including children, have a right to their opinions.

Clashes do occur. Wherever there are people, there are going to be conflicts. Wherever there are Christian people — truly Christian people — there is going to be forgiveness. Forgiveness helps to keep things going when the gears of life become stripped. Forgiveness repairs the damage. Whenever any of you has a complaint against someone else, be helpful to one another, and forgive one another. "You must forgive each other in the same way that the Lord has forgiven you." It is the Christian way; it is the only real way.

Forgiveness is Christian nobility in action. If there is criticism of the church today, this is the place where it could probably home in. There is so little understanding and forgiveness in the Christian family, and so much readiness to follow the way that comes much more naturally, the way of bitterness and recrimination.

God is good at forgiving, because He loves. We are the people of God; He loved us and chose us for His own. Let us learn to forgive, said the apostle to the church. This is what it takes to be the church, the people of God: compassion, kindness, humility, gentleness, patience, and forgiveness. "To all these add love, which binds all things together in perfect unity."

What does it take to be the church? When all is said and done, the whole thing is wrapped up in one little four-letter word: love. That takes in a lot of territory. Love accomplishes so much, and is practiced so little. Where are you going to find love if you don't find it in the church?

If anyone did something wrong, we say: "Come on in; here you will find love!" We won't tell him that what he did was right; we'll tell him that what he did was wrong. But we will also tell him that for the sake of Jesus Christ, who died for him, he is forgiven just as much as we are forgiven. We will call him and help him to a new life in Christ. This is love, strong enough to face the facts, the real hard facts of life.

There are those, men and women, who are alcoholics. Or they have been running around with others' wives and husbands. Or they are sitting in cells somewhere, paying their debt to society. Or they are just lonely because nobody cares. It doesn't make any difference. Here is love. This is the church. Here is compassion, kindness, humility, gentleness, patience, and forgiveness. Let them come in! Here is love.

Wherever the church is, there God is, and there we are all God's guests. If families go to pieces and countries tear each other apart, God is still at work in the world, inviting you to enjoy His peace in His church. Come on in and join the family, His family, your family! Come in and be thankful! Let Christ's message in all its richness live in your heart. Let it live.

5. The Church
Speaks to Decision-Makers

Before the dawn of the atomic age, when this emerging world of ours now rapidly coming into reality was still a gleam in somebody's eye, the English philosopher C. M. Joad said that people now have the power of gods but use it as irresponsibly as schoolboys. If that was true a generation ago, it is a glaring fact today. No one can ignore it, certainly not the church of Jesus Christ.

In this modern world more and more people have a part in the decisions which affect the lives of millions of their fellowmen. With certain notable exceptions, many nations of the world have given at least some of those millions a voice in the decisions which affect their welfare, along with the welfare of many others associated with them in one way or another. However, when all is said and done, with all of the participation of millions of people in the decision-making process, there are always those few who eventually have the authority and must accept the responsibility for making the hard and fast decision which will determine policy in the foreseeable future. They are, in a special sense, the decision-makers.

Let's take an example from the world of business to show how the decision-making process often works. Several years ago, mobilized and crystalized by the publication of just one book, an outcry developed from the American public regarding the lack of safety features in American-made automobiles. The problem was not that automobile manufacturers did not have competent safety engineers on their payroll. The problem was that they also had styling engineers and mechanical engineers who were interested in producing an attractive and powerful vehicle which could meet the competition from other automobile manufacturers interested in the same thing. There is just so much that you can do for a certain amount of money, and the decision-makers paid more attention to their engineers working on style and horsepower than they did to their own engineers working on safety. It was just that simple.

Apparently things are going to change. The decision-makers have decided things are going to change. One of the most notable of the decision-makers in the automobile industry told a congressional committee, "We've got the message." From now on the safety engineers will probably be listened to with the same respect formerly accorded only to those interested in style and horsepower.

Now you multiply this little example by a few thousand or so — in industry, government, education, voluntary organizations, labor unions, and even charitable enterprises — and you have a picture of human society in the modern world, especially in those countries where freedom of enterprise is still encouraged and decision-makers are still responsive to public opinion.

In the modern world there are going to be decision-makers. That is not necessarily a bad thing. It can be a very good thing. Whether you think of the millions who start the process by having the courage to say what they think or the thousands who make the ultimate decisions, it is much better to have people who think and people who are capable of making decisions than to do no thinking at all and to make no decisions at all.

We have been saying that our Lord gave the church a mission to people living in their own time, a mission that is never out of date. His followers are to proclaim the unchanged and unchanging Gospel of redemption through Jesus Christ to their own world, not to the world of their ancestors. The Good News of forgiveness and life in Christ was never so good as it is today. It is good for a world of nuclear fission, jet propulsion, space exploration, and remarkable social change. The church has a mission to this world of ours — this newly emerging world — because it has been entrusted with the Gospel of Jesus Christ, and for no other reason.

In our newly emerging society, the faint form of which we are just beginning to see, the church has a mission to a world of decision-makers. The church cannot forget where it is. Our Lord said that His people were not to be *of* the world, but they were to be right *in* the world, making their presence felt on every side.

What is that presence? St. Peter describes it quite personally and clearly: "You are God's 'chosen generation,' His 'royal priesthood,' His 'holy nation,' His 'perculiar people' — all the old titles of God's people now belong to you. It is for you now to demonstrate the goodness of Him who has called you out of darkness into His amazing light. In the past you were not 'a people' at all. Now you are the people of God. In the past you had no experience of His mercy, but now it is intimately yours.'' (1 Peter 2:9-10)

One thing is clear: In their own generation God's people are to *be* God's people — thinking as God's people, talking as God's people, acting as God's people. In a world where decision-making is an important part of community life, on whatever level, God's people are to play their part as God's people in that process. You need have no fear, said St. Peter, because you are God's people and will always be His people. He is not ashamed to be called your God, and He will show you His covenant.

The apostle was not giving the church as an institution *carte blanche,* as some people seem to think today, to enter the world of politics, government, or business as just another community organization attempting to influence decisions that have to be made. That idea might gratify some power-hungry church politicians, but it is not in this text from First Peter. It is certainly possible and sometimes appropriate for the church as an institution to make a public statement on a matter of great moral moment affecting the general public interest, but the church does not do its best and greatest work with a proliferation of statements on all kinds of questions just because they happen to be in the public eye at the moment. It is my feeling that a continuous flow of statements from the church on every conceivable subject does more harm than good. For one thing, the church comes to be regarded, sometimes even in the minds of those who are making the statements, as just another social institution exerting various pressures on public life, at best for the common good and at worst for the benefit of their own membership.

The church is not just another social institution. In the last analysis it is not an institution at all. The church is the living organism of God's people, whoever and wherever they are. God's people are those who have been called to faith in Jesus Christ in whatever nation or society they live. They are members of a family, God's family. They sit around His table as sons and daughters, recognized by their Father because they acknowledge His Son as their Savior. Because they belong to God's family in Jesus Christ, God's people belong in God's world, of which Jesus Christ is Lord. Without apology they take their place in God's world to accomplish His saving purpose in the world. They are not afraid to play that part, no matter what the world may look like. They are God's people.

I invite you to join God's people by faith in Christ. That's all it takes — faith in Christ. Christ died for you, and Christ lives for you. This is true. Christ forgives you, and Christ restores you to your proper place in the family of God. Take Him at His word. He means it. Christ renews you and gives you strength for a new life in Him. He promises it, and He will not go back on His promise. Christ is Savior and Lord. Follow Him and be the man or woman, the boy or girl He wants you to be.

All in Christ are God's chosen generation, His

royal priesthood, His holy nation, His peculiar people, redeemed by God through Christ to be God's own, to His praise and glory.

The church is not just another social institution. It is the living organism of God's living people wherever they may be. Wherever God's people are, they will be at work in the world, in the ordinary events of human life, in the whole decision-making process of modern society, demonstrating the goodness of Him who has called them out of darkness into His amazing light. This is the way God wants it to be. This is the way it *will be* if the people of the church are really God's people, redeemed by Him for His own possession.

When you talk of the church today, most people think of the Gothic building down the street or the little white frame structure on Rural Route 8. If that is the church, it will not be around when and where the decisions are being made. Those buildings are not the church!

Others think of the church as a religious institution. They talk about the Lutheran Church, or the Methodist Church, or the Roman Catholic Church. If that is the church, it will not be around when the big decisions are made in the oak-paneled offices of big business or big government.

What is the church then? Is it the individual member of the church? There are times when only one man or one woman can represent the whole church. On one day one man stood up to the whole apparatus of governmental and ecclesiastical power at Worms in Germany. Asked later how he felt that day, Martin Luther replied, "That one day I was the church." Although he said it without pride, it is true. One man can confront a world of decision-makers as the representative of the people of God. All alone, he can speak for all of them.

But this is not the way it usually works. The mission entrusted by our Lord to His church is the mission of the whole church to the whole world. Everyone has to play his part with a sense of responsibility to God and to every other member of God's family, God's chosen generation, God's royal priesthood, God's holy nation, God's own people redeemed by Him for His own possession. Everyone has a duty not just to himself but to God and to God's people — the duty to demonstrate the goodness of God, who has called His people out of darkness into His amazing light.

Every individual member of Christ is a member of Christ's body. Otherwise the word "member" has no meaning. Every member of Christ's body has a responsibility to every other member of Christ's body, no matter who he is or where he may be. Knit together, bound to one another by the cord of God's call in Jesus Christ, individual members of Christ's body encourage and support one another. They act as salt in the world, adding flavor to life and helping to keep it from going rotten. Living members of Christ's body are working members, bringing hope to a hopeless world and life to a world heading toward death. Members of Christ's body are forgiven sons and daughters of God by faith in Christ; they bring a forgiven quality to life all about them. They love as they have been loved; they care as they are cared for. They don't confine their activities to the four walls of a building. They enter the arena of the world to bring their influence to bear upon every area of life, including those where decisions are made. They bring light into darkness.

Members of Christ's body stand for Christ and stand up for Christ. They are opposed to violence in every form, even when it is asserted that violence is the only way to bring about social change. That is why they are hated by the communists and every other outfit committed to violence as a way of life. No matter! These are people of God, redeemed by God to be His own possession, expected by God to conduct themselves as His sons and daughters.

Members of Christ's body are opposed to injustice in every form. That is why they are hated by those who play upon the prejudices of other people in order to protect their own private and selfish interests. No matter! These are the people of God, redeemed by God for better things, expected by God to conduct themselves as members of His family.

Though they catch it from both sides—and sometimes from every side—members of Christ's body will demonstrate the goodness of Him who has called them out of darkness into His amazing light. How could they do otherwise, when they are the people of God, knowing that Christ, who committed no sin and was convicted of no falsehood, refused to answer abuse with abuse. When He suffered, He uttered no threats but committed His cause to the One who judges justly. In His own person He carried the sins of the world to the cross that His people might cease to live for sin and begin to live for righteousness. By the wounds of Christ His people have been healed. By His life they live to do their part in God's world, to help their fellowmen make the decisions that have to be made if people are to be benefited and God is to be honored.

God knows it is not easy to act courageously and honorably in a world where power plays such a role. Because it is not easy, the followers of Christ have not always stood for Him and have not always stood up for Him. There have been times when the followers of Christ were afraid to act as the forgiven sons and daughters of God. Great numbers of them acted as anything but members of the family of God putting their faith to work.

Some of the most pious people of God wash out on their responsibilities, giving others the impression that they are concerned only with religious matters, sometimes claiming that they do not want to meddle in human affairs. They do not reflect credit on the name of Christ, who did not hesitate to enter every aspect of human life in all of His deity, though some people may have called it meddling.

People of God who follow Christ cannot be content simply to support the status quo, to occupy a little corner of life, give a pious blessing at the beginning of a civic meeting and then leave the scene so as not to be accused of meddling. This would be to support the thesis that God is dead. God is not dead. He lives in His Son Jesus Christ and in the living body of Christ which is the church. God lives in His family, the people of God, His chosen generation, His royal priesthood, His holy nation, His people redeemed to be His own possession. God lives, and His people live with Him.

God's people don't just sit around and say, "We love, we love, we love." People who love take action. A father doesn't just sit by and let love radiate off his beaming face while his child is about to be run over by a truck in the street. He gets up and acts. He risks his life to rescue the object of his love. God's people can do no less. God so loved the world that He gave the best He had—His only Son. The people of God, who owe their fellowship with God to Jesus Christ, can do no less. Christ died for all, that they who live should not henceforth live unto themselves but unto Him who died for them and rose again.

The love of the people of God takes concrete form in considerate action within the society in which each of us lives. In the decision-making vital to that society, God's people have to be there. They have to be there as God's people, helping along, taking the hard knocks, doing the hard thinking, taking responsibility for the hard decisions that have to be made. God's people have to be ready to accept the responsibility of leadership in the worlds of business, politics, education, labor, finance, international affairs, social welfare, and charitable endeavors of every kind. They have to be willing to pay the price of leadership, which is good, hard work. Unless they do, God's people will play no role at all in this emerging world where hard decisions have to be made.

In their mission to a world of decision-makers, showing forth the goodness of Him who has called them out of darkness into His marvelous and amazing light, the people of God do not stand alone.

He is with them. What is more, the people of God have each other, to encourage one another and to help one another. With a sense of mission to our world, our rapidly emerging world, God's people will encourage one another; they will help one another.

Where do we fit into this picture? Maybe we are among those decision-makers, ultimately responsible for the hard decisions that affect many other people. If so, we won't stand aside from the people of God as if we don't belong. We associate ourself openly with the body of Christ, which is the church, and we will benefit everybody, including ourselves.

If you are one of those little people who wonder where they fit in, associate yourself openly with the people of God and with them bring influence to bear for good on life all around you. In so doing, though you may not realize it, you play a part in the decision-making process which affects all of us. Strengthen the hand of others for what is right and good! You may be just the one to cause a whole host of others at a critical moment to make the crucial decision that is right and good for everyone.

Jesus Christ is Lord. Live under His lordship, for out of the goodness of His heart He gave His life for you. Let Him exercise His lordship in your life, great or small as it may be, to help shape this emerging world of ours as He wants it to be.

6. The Unity of the Church

To those who look in from outside, what is the most impressive fact, the one they first notice, about the church which professes its faith in Christ the Savior? Is it that conviction of Christian people which in the apostolic age turned that topsy-turvy world upside down? Or is it the love of Christian people which caused their unbelieving neighbors in the apostolic age to exclaim, "Behold, how they love one another!"? In some cases, yes. But in many more, I am afraid the answer will have to be no.

Across the world, in almost every country where the church lives and works, the first, deepest, and most lasting impression it gives is one of disunity — disunity often punctuated by bitter competition, deep-seated jealousy, envy, suspicion, and conflict. Our sadly divided world is confronted by a sadly divided church, which frequently displays all the characteristics of the world to which it claims to bring salvation through the grace of God which is in Christ Jesus our Lord. We must face the hard fact that to many people outside the church Christian faith appears to conform rather than to transform. It appears that way because of Christian people or because of the Christian organizations whose attitudes they espouse and defend.

Our Lord did not intend His church to be a collection of warring sects. Nor did He visualize it as a monolithic world organization imposing its will and dogma upon the faithful through law and regulation, claiming the authority of the Holy Spirit of God for doctrines and rules that are essentially man-made.

It is the will of Christ that His church be one. This fact is very evident from a striking section of our Lord's dramatic prayer offered to His Father on the night of His betrayal and recorded in the 17th chapter of St. John:

> Sanctify them through Thy truth; Thy Word is truth. As Thou hast sent Me into the world, even so have I also sent them into the world. And for their sakes I sanctify Myself, that they also might be sanctified through the truth.
>
> Neither pray I for these alone, but for them also which shall believe on Me through their word: that they all may be one as Thou, Father, art in Me and I in Thee; that they also may be one in Us; that the world may believe that Thou hast sent Me.
>
> And the glory which Thou gavest Me I have given them, that they may be one, even as We are one: I in them and Thou in Me, that they may be made perfect in one, and that the world may know that Thou hast sent Me and hast loved them as Thou hast loved Me.
>
> Father, I will that they also whom Thou hast given Me be with Me where I am, that they may behold My glory, which Thou hast given Me; for Thou lovedst Me before the foundation of the world. O righteous Father, the world hath not known Thee, but I have known Thee, and these have known that Thou hast sent Me. And I have declared unto them Thy name and will declare it, that the love wherewith Thou hast loved Me may be in them, and I in them. (John 17:17-26)

This passage gives no comfort to those who look upon disunity in the church as a welcome, essential, or even divine characteristic of Christendom. Nor does it give any encouragement to those who would impose unity upon the church through political arrangements or organizational compromises. History has shown that this process never works, because it fails to recognize both the origin and the nature of the church's unity. Indeed, advocates both of disunity and of a regulated, imposed unity close their eyes to the origin and nature of the church itself.

Wherever the church exists — on whatever continent, in whatever country, in whatever community or locality — it is one with the church in every other place, no matter where that place may be. The church is one because Christ is one, and He cannot be divided. Christ is the Head of His church, and the church is His body. Individual believers in Christ are members of that body — that's the meaning of the word "member" — a part, an integral part, of Christ's body, attached to Him by faith and working in the only way faith works: by love.

There is one Head and one body. No man can take the place of Christ, the Head of the church. No body can be substituted for that corporate unity which is His body, consisting of the members of that body, those who recognize Christ as their Head and follow His direction.

Christ prayed that the glory which the Father had given Him might be given to the members of His body, that they might be one even as He and the Father are one: "I in them and Thou in Me, that they may be made perfect in one, and that the world may know that Thou hast sent Me and hast loved them as Thou hast loved Me.''

It should be perfectly clear that the church founded by Christ does not consist of denominations. It consists of people who truly and sincerely believe in Christ, earnestly endeavoring to follow Him and confidently looking forward to the day when they will be with Christ where He is, that they may behold His glory, which the Father has given Him.

Not everyone who belongs to a church belongs to Christ. Not everyone who talks about Christ belongs to Christ. There are those who say, ''Lord, Lord,'' in the most unctious tones, but Christ has a word for them: ''I never knew you.'' The true members of Christ's church are sanctified — set apart — by His truth. That truth is Christ's Word. Christ prayed for those who believe in Him, that they might be united in the only way in which they can be united: ''Sanctify them through Thy truth; Thy Word is truth. As Thou hast sent Me into the world, even so have I sent them into the world. And for their sakes I sanctify Myself, that they also might be sanctified through the truth. Neither do I pray for these alone, but for them also which shall believe on Me through their word: that they all may be one as Thou, Father, art in Me and I in Thee; that they also may be one in Us; that the world may believe that Thou hast sent Me.''

It is not my purpose to disparage denominations, although extravagant denominationalism has often obscured the cross of Christ. It is also true that the work of Christ is being done today largely by people who wholeheartedly support their denominations. Many of the younger churches throughout the world owe their existence to the interest taken in them by denominations in other parts of the world.

It is not my purpose to tell leaders at denominational headquarters what to do. These leaders, however, together with the members of their denominations, must not, dare not, and cannot forget that the church of Christ is not confined to any denomination, that the denomination is not an end in itself, and that God has a purpose in the world to which He calls every member of the body of Christ, no matter where he may be found. God's purpose? That the world may believe that the Father has sent Jesus Christ; that, knowing Jesus Christ, the world may inherit and enjoy the glory which the Father has given to Christ and through Christ shares with the world; that, having this glory, those who believe in Christ may proclaim the same Word by which they have been brought to faith in order that others may believe through their word.

The glory of Christ belongs to everyone who believes in Him, who accepts Him as Savior and Redeemer. That glory is offered to everyone, the glory of being a son of God through faith in Christ. It is the only glory that matters. Men who have found their glory in Christ—in Him alone—possess a relationship to each other which Christ can describe in no other way than being one. What makes them one is that they believe in the same Lord in exactly the same way, drawn by the same Spirit to the same task of letting the world know that the

Father has sent Christ, the divine Answer to the world's problem.

St. Paul said "There is one body and one Spirit . . . one Lord, one faith, one Baptism." This passage is in every Bible, no matter in what translation or in which language. Unity of the church is to be found not in what people do or have done. It lies in what God has done for us all in Jesus Christ.

About this there can be no disagreement. Unless we know what God has done for us in Jesus Christ, we do not know the elemental truth by which men are set apart to serve the Lord Christ. "Sanctify them in Thy truth," He said; "Thy Word is truth."

The Word of God is the last court of appeal, settling every argument and judging every claim. That Word tells us about Christ, whom Martin Luther called "the King and Lord of Scripture." Christ is more than a slogan. Christ's will is expressed clearly in His Word. In spite of everything you may have heard, it is impossible to interpret that Word in various ways. It means just exactly what it says. We are not supposed to read anything into it or read anything out of it. We are expected to accept it as it is. That Word is truth, and by it the followers of Christ are sanctified, set apart for faith and service.

Unity in Christendom, real unity, will have to come as faith comes in the first place — as a divine gift. We cannot bring it about by organizational compromise or even by discussing differing denominational points of view. Fraternal love, noble as it may be, cannot accomplish what God alone can do. Ecclesiastical pronouncements are not enough.

The greatest contribution we Christians can make to the development of that outward unity which will reflect the inner unity that always characterizes believers in Christ, is to pray for it. This may sound like impractical advice. Really it is the most practical advice in the world. Even Christ prayed that His followers might be one, that the world might believe that the Father had sent Him. Unless unity is a divine acheivement, there will be no unity at all.

If denominations are to have any role in Christ's plans for His church, they must constantly reexamine themselves to see whether they are really proclaiming Christ's truth and whether their denominational life is based on that truth. The thrust of Christ's truth is toward oneness — a unity that is not a mechanical process but a growth from within by the power of the Spirit of Jesus Christ. It will not do, therefore, to strive for unity on the basis of a slogan like, "We all call ourselves Christians; why can't we get together?" It will not do to try to unite Christendom by agreeing to disagree. It will not do to unite those who honor Christ with those who dishonor Him; those who accept Christ as Savior with those who believe that He is only one way to salvation; those who believe that Christ is God, with those who believe that He is just a divine being on a higher level than other human beings; those who believe in His atonement and bodily resurrection with those who regard these miracles as mere myths. Christian unity, desirable as it is to demonstrate to the world that the Father has sent Christ to be the Savior of the world, must recognize first of all that God's Word is truth. Otherwise there can be no unity.

It is my earnest and sincere prayer that Christians everywhere might acknowledge their one faith, their one Lord, and their one baptism. It is my prayer because it was Christ's prayer. Let them make it their prayer that Christians everywhere may be one in this faith, that the world may believe that the Father has sent Christ. Such prayer is very likely the greatest contribution they can make to Christian unity.

God sees to it that the things we pray for we work for. We need to pray that we may get to know Christ, that we may draw closer to Him through study of the Scriptures. The closer Christians are to Christ, the closer they will be to one another. Let our first loyalty be to Christ. Denominational loyalty is commendable, but Christ commanded us to confess Him and to witness to Him. Martin Luther once asked Christians not to be loyal to him. He said: "I did not die for anyone." Christ died for us; He commands our highest loyalty.

It is our privilege to offer gentle but firm testimony to our faith in Christ. To witness to Christ, we must be on speaking terms with the world as we are on speaking terms with Christ. To witness to other Christians, we must be on speaking terms with them as we are on speaking terms with Christ. Christ asked us to witness to our faith, not to argue about it or to fight about it. The cross of Christ is sufficient offense to the world without offering additional offense through our own ill-considered words and actions. Christ prayed the Father not to take us out of the world but to keep us from the evil that is in the world. If we are Christians, let us call upon His name and witness to His saving name.

We ought to study what other Christians believe so that we may not circulate about them our own erroneous preconceptions and prejudices. There is enough error in Christendom without creating it where it does not exist. It is not our business to win an argument but to witness to Christ.

Let us live a Christian life which will bring honor to Christ, to our church, and to our denomination. The witness of a Christian life has drawn many an unbeliever to Christ and many another Christian closer to Christ.

It will help if we show love to Christians of other denominations, even though we may feel strongly — and possibly even correctly — that they do not have as fine an understanding of the Gospel as we do. We should talk about our fellow Christians in other denominations with kindness and respect. We should put our faith in Christ into practice, remembering that there are others who believe in Christ and are sincerely endeavoring to put their faith into practice.

From what I have said, my readers may have got the idea that I do not have any great hopes for contributions to the unity of Christendom. If they have got that idea, they are right. I do not.

If they have got the idea that I, and others like me, are not interested in Christian unity, they are wrong. I cannot be a follower of Jesus Christ without praying for the unity of all those who follow Him in faith.

All of us may never belong to the same denomination. Yet if we all trust in Christ as our Savior, our Redeemer, our living Lord, we are God's children. As God's children, we should love one another as our heavenly Father has loved us in Christ. If we believe in Christ the Savior, we are brothers in the faith. Let us pray that the Spirit of God will lead us into true unity as we are sanctified in that truth which is His Word.

7. The Church:
for Sinners Anonymous

An organization calling itself Alcoholics Anonymous has been of great service to many people afflicted with alcoholism. Associated in its work are people who are themselves alcoholics and have helped each other to overcome the problem. One of the first steps in the process is to admit to themselves that they are alcoholics, completely unable to handle intoxicating liquor and therefore committed to the necessity of never touching a drop. To be helped, others have to make the same admission and to recognize the same necessity. They are encouraged to seek power from on high in order to achieve what is humanly impossible. In the fellowship created by their common problem, these people endeavor to be of constant assistance to each other. There is no sham, no condescension, no censorious attitude, only a desire to help, plus a willingness to stand by with personal presence and performance in moments of desperate need.

It is not my purpose to comment today on Alcoholics Anonymous, except to point out that it offers the only practical program I know with a real record of achievement in helping people to overcome the terrible curse of alcoholism. No other organized group of people, including the church, has been able to do as much.

This raises the question: Is the church always as aware as it should be of what it really is? Is its fellowship meaningful in the sense that it really works? What is the church anyway?

Some people have the impression that the church is a collection of high class snobs, come together for the purpose of criticizing everyone except themselves. Where do people get this impression?

The picture of the church as an assembly or even an organization of righteous people, smugly sure of themselves and bitterly critical of everyone else, certainly does not come from Jesus Christ. Our Lord felt Himself to be at home with sinners. He associated with sinners, a fact that brought Him sharp censure from certain church people of His time. The people He received and even sought out were really sinners. They were tax collectors, political grafters who had cheated people blind. Or they were women with lurid reputations, women of the streets. When no one else would talk to them, Christ came and ate with them. He was not above eating and talking with those regarded as outcasts, the scum of human society.

Jesus Christ was the personification of the divine invitation issued through the prophet Isaiah: "Come now, let us reason together, says the Lord; though your sins are like scarlet, they shall be as white as snow; though they are red like crimson, they shall become like wool." (Is. 1:18)

The Savior of men did not condone the sins of men. Brought to a cross by human sin, He could never take sin lightly. He knew the terrible blot cast on human history as well as upon individual human lives by transgression of God's will.

Note that God did not say in this case: "Though you think your sins are like scarlet, they are really not; though you think they are red like crimson, that is not the whole story." Sin is sin in God's eyes, and no one can make it out to be saintliness. In the sight of God sin is like scarlet. It is red like crimson. Our Lord knew what sin is. Yet He visited with sinners and ate with them.

Wherever the church exists, it is an assembly of people who are themselves sinners. They don't just look like sinners; they are sinners. They are not the kind of people who misjudge sin, saying, "I am not so bad, after all. I go to church and therefore my record is good." Wherever the church is doing its job, it consists of people who could very well call themselves "Sinners Anonymous." They have admitted to themselves what they are. They don't think of their own sins as being anything but scandalous. They need a Savior as much as anyone else does. If they are righteous in the sight of God, it is not because they are such good people. They know what they are, what needs to be forgiven in their lives, and how they must depend constantly upon the grace of God to meet the temptations of life.

"Sinners Anonymous" is a fellowship of people who have the same problem and the same Savior. They have found Christ to be the answer to their problem. He died for sin, and in Him there is forgiveness for sin. Forgiven people can never be the same again. They do not want to go the way they have come. They must go on to better things, strengthened by the Spirit of God, who has assured them of forgiveness in Jesus Christ.

Obviously people do not always have this picture of the church. Many of them say to themselves, "The church has no use for me. The church doesn't understand me at all. I just wouldn't feel at home in a place like that, with people like that."

Where do people get such a picture of the church? Very often from church people themselves. The church schedules fellowship programs which are superficial, shallow, and stultifying. The real issues of life are left untouched, and the deep meaning of the atonement of Christ is almost lost in the process. Someone has described the atmosphere of this so-called Christian fellowship as "bogus friendliness created by polite, superficial, and often gossipy social intercourse," leaving people with the impression that Christian fellowship is something like that of a country club, bringing people together on a Sunday morning and possibly even once or twice during the week without affecting their basic attitudes toward themselves or toward other people. Fun, food, and fellowship are often grouped together as if they were all part of the one object to which the church has dedicated itself.

The Scriptures speak of "fellowship in the Gospel," "fellowship with the Father and the Son," and "fellowship one with another" — all relationships which have to do with the greatest needs of human life and all designed to help satisfy those needs. Christian fellowship is born when God addresses Himself to sinners. It is a fellowship of sinners responding to God, who took the initiative to find a common meeting ground with men.

That common meeting ground is the cross of Jesus Christ. God says: "Come now, let us reason together; though your sins are like scarlet, they shall be as white as snow; though they are red like crimson, they shall become like wool." God means what He says. He is in dead earnest. He wants to remove whatever stands between every sinner and Himself—the sin that makes him a sinner. To do this, He sent His own Son to be a "sinner." He made Him, who knew no sin at all, to be sin for us that we sinners might be made the righteousness of God in Him.

The members of Alcoholics Anonymous say to each other, "I know what you are. I was in the gutter myself." It is pretty evident that no one talks to a man wrestling with the problem of alcoholism as well as that man who has wrestled with the same problem and has found its solution.

No one can talk to a sinner wrestling with his problem and the emptiness of life it brings as well as that sinner can who has wrestled with the same problem and has found its solution. The church has never been made up of saints with shining halos. It has always consisted of ordinary people, battling with sin and selfishness, finding the solution to their problem in the grace of a God who forgives without thought of repayment because there is no possibility of repayment. Christ drank the last drop of human misery resulting from human sin. Nothing remains to be done except to trust Him, to accept the gift of forgiveness, and to love the Giver.

God finds sinners where they are. He forgives them on the spot. There is no meeting God halfway. He has taken hold of the situation Himself and has torn down the wall serving as a barrier to access with Himself. He has done everything. The ground at Calvary, where He showed His hand once and for all, is the only common meeting ground for sinners to meet their God. There He washes them white as snow though their sins are like scarlet; there He fashions into the whitest wool what was red like crimson.

There is no such thing as being half saved or half forgiven. It is either-or. Either you belong to God or you don't. Either you are a sinner who has been cleansed or you are still in your old state of sin. This is the way it is.

No man who has ever met God at the meeting ground of Christ's cross can ever be proud of himself. He can never take a righteous or censorious attitude toward other people. He just can't, because he is a member of "Sinners Anonymous." He is bound to help wherever there is need for help. He simply must do for others what others have done for him. This is the picture of the church we receive in the New Testament.

The commitment of early Christians was to Christ. This commitment was evident in their fellowship. Each of them was his brother's keeper. These early Christians loved to help to a degree almost unknown in Christian communities today. To them the church was not a building down the block but a Christian fellowship enjoyed with others in the same boat.

We Christians are in the same boat with sinners the world over. We are followers of Him who told the story of the Pharisee and the tax collector. While the Pharisee was thanking God that he wasn't a sinner, the tax collector openly acknowledged that he had no claim on God because he was a sinner. All he could do was plead for mercy. Jesus said it was this poor sinner who went home justified.

Christ was not satisfied just to tell stories. He visited the home of Zacchaeus, a tax collector. This man had been a real scoundrel, a swindler of the first rank. But Jesus went to his home in order to bring him to the love and mercy of God. Zacchaeus was so overjoyed at this unexpected consideration, this mark of love, that he gave back to those from whom he had stolen more than they had lost, and of his remaining goods he gave half to the poor. He had become a member of "Sinners Anonymous," that great company to which all belong who have been cleansed by the scarlet, crimson blood of Christ, shed for the remission of a world's sin.

To what do we belong if we belong to a church? What are we joining if we are joining a church? We don't belong to anything unless we belong to "Sinners Anonymous." We are not joining anything unless we join "Sinners Anonymous." This is God's company, His community, His fellowship, His church.

Some of us are probably shopping around for a "nice church" to join. Instead of looking for a cathedrallike building and a beautiful, superb choir, why not look for the place where we can say, "We came here because we are looking for the forgiveness and help only God can give"? If we say that to the minister, and after he has recovered from the shock, he will probably grasp our hand to wring it warmly, if he doesn't actually embrace us. A real minister of the Gospel always has this feeling about his congregation: "These people are sinners. They know that by themselves they cannot lick sin. In their heart of hearts they know how easy it is to deny God. They are here to be reminded of His forgiveness, to receive His strength, and to take a new hold on hope." He wishes that the people in his congregation were all aware of the fact that they are members of "Sinners Anonymous," that is, people ready to help others in the way they have been helped.

Let me say something first of all to church members. Those who profess the name of Christ can help to make the church what it ought to be — not a prize collection of respectability but the assembly of the redeemed, who never forget from what they have come and toward what by the grace of God they are going. The redeemed can never be indifferent to sin, and they can never be indifferent to sinners. It is our privilege to accept others as God has accepted us. We don't stand by doing nothing when we see someone faltering, or misguided, or plunging toward destruction. We have a care as God has a care for us.

We have a care for people inside and outside the church — even for those who don't want to have anything to do with the church. All Christians have to grasp this one fact: The mercy of God which has turned the scarlet into white and the crimson into wool is great enough to include all. We don't have to build a false front. It includes us. If it includes us, it can include anyone. Christians can never assume that anyone is beyond the reach of the Gospel of the grace and glory of God in Jesus Christ.

Now let me say something to those who have been thinking about going to church for the first time, or for the first time in a long time. Go. Don't wait. Keep on going. Don't give up. Join the fellowship — the fellowship of sinners redeemed by the Son of God and the Savior of the world.

No special qualifications are required except that we drop our pretenses. We don't have to be what we are not. We are just ourselves. God has His hand out for us in the invitation: "Come now . . . says the Lord; though your sins are like scarlet, they shall be white as snow; though they are red like crimson, they shall become like wool." The invitation is engraved with the name of the Savior, who gave His life for us. This is all we need. "Come Now!" says the Lord.

8. The Praying Church

Ever since the church's beginning, wherever there have been disciples of Jesus Christ, wherever the church is really the church, it has been a praying church. Strong men pray. They don't have to be afraid to pray. Lovely women pray. It is beautiful to pray. Boys and girls pray. They have a Friend who wants them to have joy. "Amen and amen," He said, "whatsoever ye shall ask the Father in My name, He will give it you. . . . Ask and ye shall receive, that your joy may be full." (John 16:23-24)

Prayer is not the dreary exercise so many people have made it out to be. When down and out, they pray; not otherwise. When they feel sorry for themselves, they pray; not otherwise. When their hopes for glory or advancement or happiness don't turn out, suddenly they turn to prayer; not otherwise.

Jesus Christ understood people in trouble. He knew all about trouble Himself. But He could never understand why people don't pray, whether they are in trouble or not. He knew His Father, and He turned to Him in time of trouble. He knew His Father, and He turned to Him all the time.

Knowing God is a great thing. When the Son of God came, as He did, He kept telling people, "My Father knows Me, and I know Him." This is not something for theologians to argue about. It's a practical fact of great importance to every man alive. Jesus Christ knew God as His Father.

Jesus Christ came not just to show us the Father but to hook every one of us up to God. He suffered, the just One for all of the unjust ones, to bring us to God. He put out of the way the hostility, the stubbornness, and the fear that make people want to get away from God. While we were yet enemies, Christ died for us; now by His life we are saved. "Believe it and be saved, every one of you." That's what His men kept saying to people. It's what we keep on saying today.

God speaks, and people don't listen. Then they wonder why He isn't listening when all of a sudden they get the urge to pray. You would almost think that man was doing God a favor by praying to Him. That's what a lot of people seem to think. "I prayed," someone writes to me, "and God wasn't listening." I believe it.

Communication in business, in school, or in marriage, as anybody knows, is a two-way street. If you want somebody to listen to you, you have to be ready to listen to him. If you have just got a vacant stare in your eyes when he speaks to you, it is almost an insult to expect him to listen whenever you open your mouth. You talk to him only when you want to take him for all he is worth. If I read the Bible correctly, God is not stupid. He knows what the score is. You don't have to tell Him, and you can't take Him in. You can't take Him in with that little confidence game, pretending to do Him a favor by throwing Him a prayer now and then.

What good is a telephone in your home if it isn't hooked up to the lines? You can call till you're blue in the face and won't get anything at all. You won't even get a dial tone. That's what a lot of people are complaining about when they say, "I prayed, and He didn't listen."

Jesus Christ puts things together again. He hooks everything together in heaven and on earth. He died to bring forgiveness for all, friends and enemies. He lives to heal all the hurt. Christ died for all of us, whoever we are. Let's listen to Him and trust Him. He is for us. With Him strangeness disappears, and a new friendship begins — friendship with God, believe it or not. It's ours to have and enjoy by faith in Jesus Christ.

It's what Jesus Christ was talking about when He said, "Truly, truly, I say to you." He swears it. "If you ask anything of the Father, He will give it to you in My name." As it were He says: "Maybe you haven't asked anything in My name before this time; try it and you will see. Ask and you will receive. Ask, receive, and find out what joy is all about."

Dr. Coburn tells about a young father who sat with his face set and grim through the funeral service for his 4-year-old son who had died of polio. As the man heard the opening words of the service, "I know that my Redeemer lives," he was heard to mutter under his breath, "God, I'll get back at You for this. I'll get back at You." That's authentic. I've heard people talk that way myself. Overcome by terrible tragedy, they suddenly come face to face with a fact of life they had hitherto ignored. Like it or not, you have got to deal with God. You can try to get away from Him, but you won't succeed. You may not know Him, but you know that He is there.

The young father didn't know it at the moment, but he was closer to God right then than he had been for a long time. Later on this same young father said: "It was a foolish thing to say, I suppose. How could I ever get back at God? But it was honest. It was the way I felt, and it cleared the atmosphere to get it all off my chest. When I came to myself, I saw that death does have to fit into some kind of a framework and only God can absorb that. In time I came to know His mind. I know now that my Redeemer does live."

A lot of people aren't angry with God at all. They just don't care about God. The whole style and pace of modern life keeps people so occupied they don't have any time for God, at least so they think. Actually most of these people are caught in the crisis of faith. They would like to believe in God, but they don't think they can. They think: "You are not quite a man if you believe in God. To admit that you need God's help isn't quite worthy of a modern man. If you concede that God cares about you, you have got to care about Him." And that goes against the grain of anyone who has been taught to believe only in himself.

It is popular today to call upon science in support of this selfish independence, as if science had somehow destroyed God or rendered Him helpless. But science hasn't done any such thing. People who don't pray because they think it is unscientific are just out of style and out of date. At one time science may have been condescending or even antagonistic to a spiritual view of life. It may have discouraged prayer. But this is not true today. I know distinguished men of science, leaders in the field, who don't feel that it is in the least bit beneath them to take Jesus Christ at His word: "If you ask the Father for anything in My name, He will give it you." Up to this time, maybe, you haven't asked anything in His name; ask and you will receive, that your joy may be full.

The former dean of the School of Science at Massachusetts Institute of Technology, Dr. George Harrison, said that the universe appeared to him to be more like a great thought than like a great thing. When you are talking about a great thought instead of a great thing, you are talking about God.

When Harrison Salisbury of the *New York Times* returned from Russia he reported that although dialectical materialism was the official creed of the communistic regime there, he found no atheists among Russia's leading men of science. Men of science are not going to be satisfied with the easy, brittle answers which have been so characteristic of the modern age. If you have got to know, eventually you are going to run head on into God.

Dr. Alexis Carrel, a great man of science and also a man of great spirit, wrote in the days of World War II:

Today, lack of emphasis on the religious sense has brought the world to the edge of destruction. Our deepest source of power and perfection has been left miserably undeveloped. Prayer, the basic exercise of the spirit, must be actively practiced by men and nations . . . . True prayer is a way of life; the truest life is literally a way of prayer . . . only in prayer do we achieve that complete and harmonious assembly of body, mind, and spirit which gives the frail human reed its unshakable strength. . . . When we pray we link ourselves with the inexhaustible motive power that spins the universe.

God is not just a force. He feels, and feels deeply. That you see in Jesus Christ. That is what Jesus Christ came to show the world. God is like a father whose children have gone wrong. He is offended, and He will do something about it. He will do everything to get them straightened out. He will give of Himself, if that's what it takes, to bring them back. He will go through the agony of putting Himself in their place, of doing for them what they cannot do for themselves, redeeming them from their willfulness and waywardness. That's Jesus Christ. There you have it. All of God's forgiveness and all of the life He has to give is in Jesus Christ. All of His fatherly heart is in Jesus Christ. In Jesus Christ He invites each of us to be one again with Him, our Father, our God.

In Jesus Christ God invites us to pray to Him. "Come on," He says, "in Christ pray. Instead of worrying about your problem, pray about it. What's the good of worrying? Pray!"

It's really quite the reverse of the question most people are asking themselves: "What's the good of praying?" Then they proceed to worry themselves to death as if there were any value in worrying. Christ's men learned the joy of praying. "Cast all your cares upon Him, for He will take care of you," one of them said. He had found it out for himself.

That's the way it works. If you trust God, the Father of our Lord Jesus Christ, you deal a death blow to all of those worries. "Amen, amen" said Jesus Christ, "I say to you, whatever you ask the Father in My name, He will give it to you. Ask and you will receive, that your joy may be full."

What Jesus Christ was really saying is this: "I know My Father, and He knows Me. Come to the Father in My name, My redeeming name, and you will find Him to be a Father too. He has a big heart for you, something you will have to find out for yourself. You find it out when you pray to Him. In the freedom you have, since forgiveness is yours in My name, and life is yours in My name, ask Him and see. Do that, and you will find joy."

Prayer is like flexing our spiritual muscles. If we haven't been exercising them lately, we may find it a little painful at first. We begin by being honest with ourselves. We don't pretend or try to cover up. We act natural with God. He is not impressed with our piety or our powers of expression. We are ourselves. "Ask," said Jesus, "ask Him in My name, and you will receive."

To my readers I say: Be natural! Be yourself! There is no special religious language. Use your words. If you were on the telephone with God, what would you say? You might feel a little flustered at first, with Him on the other end of the line. But there He is. Talk to Him. Talk to Him about the things that have been worrying you, the things that have been eating at you, the things you would like to get off your chest. Talk to Him about yourself.

There is nothing wrong about that. Talk to Him about others. Mention them by name. Let Him know that you have the courage to talk to Him because you have confidence in His Son Jesus Christ. It's good for you to remember, and it pleases Him to hear you say it. Whatever you ask the Father in His name, that great Son of His has told you the Father will give it to you. "Ask and you will receive, that your joy may be full."

We have freedom in prayer. We feel free to say what we think. We feel free to use the prayer of someone else if we want to, if it says what we want to say. Sometimes the poets say things for us, things we feel deeply ourselves. We need not hesitate to quote them. The psalms from the Bible have been the prayer book of the church down through the ages. There are all kinds of psalms. There are also songs and hymns, some of them good and some of them not so good, some of them great poetry and some of them not so great, offered to God by people who felt deeply in the past. The church is glad to have them. They help the church to pray. Wherever the church is, it is a praying church.

Maybe some of you have never been in a church before, and you wonder why you should go now. To pray, that's why! Wherever people pray with one another in the name of Jesus, the Spirit of God is at work there. Some people there hear God speaking to them, and they pray to Him. It is a moving thing to pray with people like that. If anyone is afraid that God is going to get hold of him, he shouldn't go. If he wants to have joy instead of all that gloom, that dreariness, that utter barrenness of life without

God, then he should go. Let him not be afraid. The only obligation he has is to God.

I have met many people who claim to know God but seldom if ever pray to Him. Let me say quite bluntly: That's not knowing God. People like that may know about Him, but they don't really know Him.

There is no substitute for knowing God. That's where the joy comes in, knowing Him and having Him as our Friend, being sure of His forgiveness, looking to Him for what is really good in life, trusting Him to see things through, enjoying His presence, His nearness, His help. If any man is in Christ, that's what he has. He is like a new man, with new life, new hopes, new dreams. Indeed he has got new wants, new desires, and a new power for victorious living — all from knowing God by faith in Jesus Christ.

Let none say that this can't happen to him. It can happen to anyone If I can have it, everyone can have it too. He is talking to each one of us: "Amen and amen. Whatever you ask the Father in My name, He will give it to you. If you have not asked before, ask now, and you will receive, that your joy may be full."

Let's not put it off until a better time. There won't be a better time than right now. We take Christ at His word. His Word is good. We ask in His name, and we will receive. In the asking and in the receiving we will find joy.

We pray for ourselves and for others, praying to God in the name of Jesus Christ. If we pray in the atoning name of Jesus Christ, accepting Him as our

Savior and receiving His forgiveness, at that moment we are members of His church. That is His church—the assembly of those throughout the world who trust Him and call upon His name.

9. Mission
in the Local Church

More than 60,000,000 Americans today live in the suburbs, the largely residential communities surrounding larger cities. Eight out of every 10 new homes built in the United States during a recent summer were in the suburbs. The same thing is happening in every part of the world. Suburban communities have seen spectacular growth as millions move from the old and crowded conditions of the city to the adjacent countryside. Today one out of four Americans lives in the suburbs. It is estimated that the ratio will soon climb to one out of three. The urbanized world is rapidly becoming suburbanized.

Suburbia is under heavy attack today from various sides. Caustic criticism has been heaped upon suburban life as a leafy utopia of "look-alike houses occupied by act-alike people." Suburbanites have been pictured as social criminals who have escaped the problems of the city to live in their own smug and selfish isolation. Yet this way of life is the dream of virtually every American, and it has become the ultimate hope of most people in the world.

The great God, who passes judgment upon the world and all its works, sends His church on a mission to the world of today, not the world of yesterday. He speaks His word of judgment and grace to men everywhere, including those who call suburbia their home and look upon their local suburban church as their home church.

Let's face it: Many of these suburban people have "arrived" in the eyes of the world. They are well educated. They possess social skills of various kinds. Some have advanced to positions of leadership in the world of business. They have money. They have influence. They have power. They are in a position where it is easy to forget God and to settle for the little gods of this world. They are in a position to do great good, and often they use their position to perpetuate great evils. The Word of God has something to say to that situation.

St. Paul was characteristically straightforward and direct when he talked to people, including those calling themselves Christians, who have acquired a great deal and think they have everything:

> Those who desire to be rich fall into temptation, into a snare, into many senseless and hurtful desires that plunge men into ruin and destruction. For the love of money is the root of all evils. It is through this craving that some have wandered away from the faith and pierced their hearts with many pangs.
>
> But as for you, man of God, shun all this; aim at righteousness, godliness, faith, love, steadfastness, gentleness. Fight the good fight of faith; take hold of the eternal life to which you were called when you made the good confession in the presence of many witnesses. In the presence of God, who gives life to all things, and of Christ Jesus, who in His testimony before Pontius Pilate made the good confession, I charge you to keep the

commandment unstained and free from reproach until the appearing of our Lord Jesus Christ; and this will be made manifest at the proper time by the blessed and only Sovereign, the King of kings and Lord of lords, who alone has immortality and dwells in unapproachable light, whom no man has ever seen or can see. To Him be honor and eternal dominion. Amen.

As for the rich of this world, charge them not to be haughty nor to set their hopes on uncertain riches but on God, who richly furnishes us with everything to enjoy. They are to do good, to be rich in good deeds, liberal and generous, thus laying up for themselves a good foundation for the future, so that they may take hold of the life which is life indeed. (1 Tim. 6:9-19)

In this letter to Timothy St. Paul pronounces the judgment of God on a notable quality of modern life—its materialism. A lot of people don't like that kind of talk. They do not think of themselves as materialists. "Materialism" is a dirty word to them; they prefer to describe what they are seeking as "comfortable living" or "the good life." The suburbanite today wants the best of everything, whether this be color TV or the latest lawn mower. Even the secular critics of suburban life point out that its chief characteristic is material abundance. Living as they do in a prolonged period of material abundance and prosperity, suburbanites have dreams and visions of the future that know no limits. They live surrounded by an unbelievable array of appliances and gadgets—all of which come quickly to be considered as necessities: television and air conditioning, deep freezes and fun cars, electric dishwashers and backyard swimming pools, automatic dryers and the latest automatic cameras. To make sure that their moods are in tune with their gadgets, they see to it that the larder is well stocked with liquor, and the medicine cabinet has a generous supply of pep pills and tranquilizers.

The disturbing thing about all of this is that somehow it does not bring happiness. There are as many divorces among these people who have everything as there are among people who have nothing — frequently more divorces among them than among people who struggle to make a living. The rainbow is there, but the pot of gold at the end of the rainbow somehow always eludes their grasp. Each new purchase holds out the dream of making life different — somehow richer or more exciting. Still the restless quest goes on. Repeated disappointments fail to dampen their enthusiasm: "Just a little more money . . . if only we had one more room . . . if only we could live in a slightly better neighborhood . . . if only we could get a new car — maybe a convertible . . . if we could have one of those new refrigerators . . ." And so the frenzied pace down the long hill of life continues, picking up speed as it goes.

Those who are running begin to age. They grow slightly cynical. It takes bigger and bigger things to provide even a little excitement. But the basic optimism about happiness in the acquisition of more and more wealth, of more and more things, continues its pull upon their heartstrings. Finally their stories end, one by one . . in a lonely, fashionable funeral. They die with only one consolation: Their children now can take up the same race with the same goals for their generation.

It is a vicious cycle. St. Paul says so: "Those who desire to be rich fall into temptation, into a snare, into many senseless and hurtful desires that plunge men into ruin and destruction. For the love of money is the root of all evil. It is through this craving that some have wandered away from the faith and pierced their hearts with many pangs."

Avarice and selfishness have their rewards, like the reward of a mouse that gets the cheese with which the mousetrap has been baited. At this point, more likely than not, it is too late to recognize that the ceaseless search was not worth it.

St. Paul was a realist. What he was talking about you can see happening right before your eyes. The need for more things to buy happiness keeps even moderately wealthy families on the brink of financial ruin. To keep up every year more wives are taking jobs outside the home. More and more men are desperately moonlighting to provide for their families. Suburbia, which looks at first so financially secure, turns out to be constructed on the brink of a precipice. Too frequently suburbia turns out to be a debtor's paradise. Tensions are built in. Everything is purchased over longer periods of time. Anything can be afforded as long as the low monthly payments can be squeezed into the budget.

St. Paul had nothing against people working hard to improve themselves. He was not against living in the suburbs. Neither am I. I live in a suburb myself. But I am very conscious of the fact that some of the values created by suburban life in the modern world become ends in themselves, to be achieved at all costs, even at the price of forgetting what life is really all about. Though they ought to know better, people who think they have everything easily forget about God, who gave them life and redeemed their life from destruction. They forget about Christ, who gave His life for the life of the world that men everywhere might live in the secure knowledge of His forgiveness and might understand themselves as sons and daughters of God who need to rely upon Him by faith in Christ, not really living unless they have a real heart for their fellowmen as Christ had a heart for us all.

What happens when people forget about God and turn away from His grace and mercy offered so freely to the world in Jesus Christ? Life becomes a great big bore. Boredom creates an increased pressure to buy new things. These gadgets give momentary release from monotony. The increased leisure provided by the gadgets results in even greater boredom. It is a vicious cycle, an endless round of life built on a bottomless love for things. Tell those people, said St. Paul, that life is no good without God. It is a snare, a trap, leading to all kinds of senselessness that eventually plunges men into ruin and destruction. The love of money—and the endless struggle to get it—leads only to hopelessness and to outright pain.

Instead encourage these people to fight the good fight of faith, to get out of the rat race of riches and fight for something worthwhile. Tell them to aim at righteousness, godliness, faith, love, steadfastness, gentleness. Let them take hold of eternal life, to which everyone is called by Jesus Christ, who stood up to Pontius Pilate, to the whole panoply of power, and gave Himself for the good of the world.

If they do that, they will have something to live for. Tell them this: Live for God, who gives life to all things, and follow His way, free of the burden of guilt and free to keep His commandments clean and above reproach until the final coming of our Lord Jesus Christ. He will come as He promised, in God's own good time, as the blessed Controller of all things, the King over all kings, and the Master of all masters, the only Source of immortality, the One who lives in unapproachable light, the One whom no mortal eye has ever seen or ever can see. To Him be power and honor forever and ever.

Following Christ, as St. Paul said, leads to a life that is real and genuine. The temptation to live for things is put in its proper place. No longer is it necessary for suburban wives and mothers to feel unwanted and unnecessary. No longer do men and women have to seek some satisfaction in an aimless round of social activities which slowly lose their luster. It is hard for people who have nothing to understand how people who have everything become bored and jaded with life. To many it is not hard to understand at all. Life without God easily becomes the kind of existence where people find their solace in gin—in martinis all day long, from morning to night.

For many suburbanites life will not be real and genuine until they learn to say no to themselves and no to their children.

An oversupply of things often results in parental indulgence of children. Suburbia has become almost a child-centered world—"everything for the kids," as they say. If you ask the average suburbanite why he moved to the suburbs, the chances are that he will reply, "For the sake of the children." Today 27 precent of all the children in the United States live in suburbia. When asked to explain this phenomenon, a St. Louis psychiatrist said: "The suburbs are places where we would have liked to live in our own childhood. I'm convinced that many parents can't say no because they have identified themselves with their children. It's like saying no to themselves. I think it's the childhood dream gone wild."

Saying no is not enough. Following Christ calls for a big yes—yes to God. Saying yes to God and meaning it is saying yes to life itself.

People who have been engaged in what they call "the struggle for existence," trying to satisfy their deepest needs with a mounting supply of mere things, ought to get wise to themselves! They aren't in any race at all. They are just in a downhill plunge to the inevitable and meaningless end of that road. "There is a way that seemeth right unto a man, but the end thereof are the ways of death." (Prov. 16:25)

We are challenged to get in the race as people of God. There is a real battle to be fought by men and women with faith in Jesus Christ, aiming at righteousness, godliness, faith, love, steadfastness, and that sturdy gentleness which makes a man a gentleman and a woman someone to be admired.

"I charge you," said St. Paul to this young pastor,

Timothy, "that you tell people these things." There is a role for pastors today—that they be real pastors, not just fund raisers but "man raisers," setting the sights of their people on the true goals of life lived in the faith and fellowship of Christ, as it must be lived if life is to be truly satisfying to anyone.

I am convinced that people want straight talk today from their pastors. They want pastors to be men of God proclaiming the life-giving Gospel of Jesus Christ to people right where they are, not where their fathers or grandfathers were. Let pastors pronounce the judgment of God upon the wayward-ness and willfulness of men right where they are. Let them draw them to the cross of Christ, where they must be if they are to find true fulfillment of their destiny as sons and daughters of the living God. Let them talk to them about what a Christian must be in this modern world, which is so full of pride and prejudice, so given to racial tensions and class-consciousness, so eager to search for the meaning of life in the quest for things.

Christians don't hesitate to talk about money. The way a man uses his money is the clearest indication there is of what kind of man he is. Let's show people who want to fulfill their mission in life how to do it so that they may be rich in good deeds, liberal and generous, laying up for themselves a good foundation for the future, so that they may take hold of the life which is life indeed.

There is an old story by John Ruskin about a man who tried to swim to safety from a wrecked ship. Because he couldn't bring himself to leave his money behind, he tied about his waist a belt containing 200 pounds in gold. Unable to reach shore because of the extra weight, he sank and drowned. Ruskin asked, as he was sinking, "Had he the gold or had the gold him?" We ask ourselves in all honesty, "Have we got life, or has life got us?" Now is the time. We can't put it off. In Christ we lay hold of life which is life indeed.

10. The Happy Church

Most people don't expect to find joy in the church. The church is supposed to be a gloomy place, or at least a solemn place. Religious people are known more for their long faces than for the brightness of their smiles. Religious people are expected to be serious people. Who can be profound and jump for joy at the same time?

"I can," said St. Paul. "When we were still helpless, Christ died for the wicked, at the time God chose. It is a difficult thing for someone to die for a righteous person. It may be that someone may dare to die for a good person. But God has shown us how much He loves us: It was while we were still sinners that Christ died for us! By His death we are now put right with God; how much more, then, will we be saved by Him from God's wrath. We were God's enemies, but He made us His friends through the death of His Son. Now that we are God's friends, how much more will we be saved by Christ's life!" (Rom. 5:6-10). Those are mighty profound thoughts. They led this man to a mighty conclusion: "That is not all," he said. He goes on: "We rejoice in God." We exult in God, we glory in God through our Lord Jesus Christ, by whom we have got this atonement, from whom we have received reconciliation, who has now made us God's friends.

I can almost see Paul telling people in his time about Jesus Christ He is not the little, dark, scowling, and bitter religionist that some people have made him out to be. At one time he might have been that, but not now! He might still be little and dark, but not scowling and bitter. There is a friendliness in his approach which does not remind you of a con man trying to take people in. There is an attractiveness about him, a politeness in his eye, a sunny expression on his face, and a warmth in his voice. Something has happened to him, you see: He has found Jesus Christ, and that changes everything. "We jump for joy in God through our Lord Jesus Christ," he kept saying, "by whom we have now received the great thing, the atonement for our sins, reconciliation with God, and friendship with our Father, once alienated by our sins and now reconciled to us by the death of His Son. We joy in God through our Lord Jesus Christ. In Him we have got the greatest, which is atonement."

When you look around you in the church these days, you have to say to yourself: People certainly must have forgotten something. The people in the church are often so gloomy, so hostile to others and even to one another, so suspicious of everyone, so eager to find fault rather than to forgive, so solemn, so whisperingly quiet, so afraid to let themselves go, so unhappy. It isn't a happy church, not from where I sit, nor, I imagine, from where most of you sit either. What's happened? Why, people have forgotten something. They don't believe it themselves, and they don't tell it to others. They hide behind walls, for fear that someone is going to get to them. They are on the defensive, and that's always bad. It means you aren't sure of yourself;

you begin to wonder what's coming next. You fear the worst.

The worst could come, said St. Paul, and I don't care. I've got something that will carry me through thick and thin. What can bother me if God is for me? If God is for us, who can be against us? The God who gave us His own Son surely is not going to withhold from us any good thing. In this world of ours, come life, come death, come anything, He is our Friend. By His death Christ dealt with the great issues of life and of death. He overcame, and now in Him there is only life. That being the case, we joy in God through our Lord Jesus Christ, by whom we have now received this magnificent atonement.

A friend of mine told me recently that he and a number of other friends were sitting around drinking coffee and talking. "You know," said one man, "I think the pastor last Sunday was trying to tell us that we are not as happy as we should be. I have been thinking the same thing," he said. "I think he is right. If we really took seriously all of God's promises, we would be happy — and we would show it more." The second one commented, "There are all of these problems pressing in on people. It has colored our whole mood. I think of the Vietnam War grinding on; business is not improving in our area; college kids are disillusioned, even with the value of their own education; more and more groups are fighting day and night to grab off more and more power. To be happy today you almost have to be ignorant or stupid."

If you go around ignoring the evil in the world, the problems people have, the racial hatreds and the personal hostilities, the poverty all over the world and the degradation that often goes with it, the violence that results in bloodshed and the malice that inserts a knife in the back, the plain out-and-out brainlessness and heartlessness of our world — if you ignore all of that, I suppose you can be happy after a fashion. That happiness is going to be terribly superficial. Some day, sooner or later, it is going to receive a rude awakening.

I have seen people crack up and go to pieces when a boy or girl of theirs went wrong, bringing embarrassment and even disgrace upon the family. They adored their children, putting all their eggs in that one basket. When that dream exploded, their whole world blew up with it. I have seen the same thing happen to a man who put all his eggs in the basket of business. The business failed in spite of all his best efforts, and he committed suicide. Happiness can be a mighty fragile thing — here today and gone tomorrow.

Many people confuse happiness with pleasure. For them happiness is a good steak dinner, two weeks on a South Sea island, having the cute blonde down the hall smile at you, winning a new car in a contest, being young, fighting hard, enjoying life, and having pleasure. One day, all of a sudden, you begin to get pains across the chest, or a good friend lets you down, or your company merges with another company with the loss of a few crucial jobs, including your own. Then the whole picture changes. Happiness goes right out the window.

Gerald Cragg described what St. Paul was talking about in his description of the early church:

It was this exultant quality in the early Christians that so much impressed and puzzled their pagan neighbors. It was different from anything that marked ordinary human life. Pleasure is one thing; joy is another. Pleasure, when chosen wisely and used in moderation, may do much to mitigate the rigors of experience; but it can never create the atmosphere with which joy surrounds the man who has found it. Pleasure is ephemeral, usually awakened for the moment by some external stimulus, and as transient as the cause which called it forth. Joy has an enduring quality; it is a state sustained by abiding sources of spiritual renewal, and "no man taketh" it from us. It is inseparable from a discovery of a proper relationship to God. In dependence on God we discover the secret of creative power and we master the disciplines of humble and happy service. Independence in Him — that's the way. That is why we "rejoice in God"; the religious man is persuaded that only in Him can we find the wellspring of joy. The Christian is equally sure that there is no way of attaining the requisite fellowship with God except through Jesus Christ. Apart from Christ we lack the knowledge of God which enables us to "exult." He has not only shown us the Father, but He has made possible that reconciliation without which there can be no joy.

Our modern world has unthinkingly incorporated a fatal error in its thinking, namely, that modern life has outgrown its need for God and the religious interpretation of life. Taking science as the key model, modern man claims that slowly he is gaining greater mastery over life. He is being freed from former bondages. Finally he will know a human quality of life that has never been achieved in the past.

That kind of thinking has infected the church, too. Many leaders of churches, both pastors and people, have a secular view of life in which the role of God has become almost nonexistent. They go through religious forms, it is true, but God is pretty far away. What actually happens is not so much that God becomes unimportant but that man loses his way. The sons and daughters of this modern secular man are turning frantically to mysticism, drugs, all kinds of outlandish religious experience, communes — almost anything at all — to find some meaning in life, some ground to stand on, some purpose to pursue.

When it comes right down to it, this is the reason for the unhappiness in the modern world, where people were supposed to be happier than they had ever been before. Man has cut himself off from the source of joy. Joy is there, just as it always has been, but man can't seem to find it. It isn't so much that he can't but that he won't. He doesn't want to find it.

People fight God. Previous generations did it and found only unhappiness. People do it today, people like us. We fight God off. We hold Him off at arm's length, we try to get along without Him. We treat God as if He were an outmoded idea which we somehow have outgrown. We do that, and we are losers. If the truth is to be known, without God and without hope in the world we are born losers.

As Langdon Gilkey wrote recently, "The whence

of our deepest private and interior fears and the anatomy of our most frantic, foolish, and vicious public behavior remain in darkness, and we are left the vulnerable prey of demons we know not of." All of a sudden we are beginning to wake up to our lostness, our lack of someone to believe in, our failure to find joy. I begin to see signs in all of this unrest, this dissatisfaction, this desperation, that young people and older people too are beginning to look for what is real — real faith, real love, real joy.

Where are you going to find that real faith, real love, and real joy if you don't find it in the church? How are you going to find it in the church if it's not there? How can it be there if the church has no real grip on God, if it doesn't know and love Jesus Christ, if it no longer has and proclaims forgiveness and life through the atonement of the Son of God — if joy in these realities has been given up for some other moral or ethical philosophy which produces tidy but only temporary results?

To know joy, I must know what life is all about. Then I can live while things go wrong on its surface. I can bear the load when things collapse. I can keep on going even when my heart threatens to stop.

I know. I know Jesus Christ. I have got something great from Him. The great thing is atonement. It is something He did, not I. He atoned for my sins, and I am forgiven. He has power on earth to forgive sins, to make things right with God, to put my feet on solid ground, and to send me on the good way. He has all that, and He shares it with me when I go with Him.

Forgiveness always involves sacrifice. Anybody

101

who has ever forgiven knows that. It takes some doing, a reorganization of the heart, almost like giving up one's self in favor of someone else.

Forgiveness is not just that everything is going to be all right. Here is a drunken driver responsible for wiping out an entire family. Look at the eyes of that crowd as they pick up the mutilated bodies. No one there is inclined to mumble words about everything being all right. Men inflict suffering, often on the innocent. Only One who was innocent of all sin could take that ultimate suffering for sin, pay the price of its guilt, and endure the terrible effect of it on all of humanity. Only One could do that.

You can't be sentimental about forgiveness, and you can't be sentimental about the cross of Jesus Christ. The Bible speaks about healing and reconciliation. It is talking about the cross of Jesus Christ. There He died. Atonement was made. He died for all. I guess that means me. If it means me, it means everyone. He died for everyone as if that person were the only one in the whole world.

The moping, sad, and frustrated church — the one that doesn't know the meaning of atonement — doesn't know how to proclaim forgiveness. If it doesn't know how to do that, how can it bring joy to the world? There isn't anything our world needs more today than a church that is happy in its faith, happy in its love, happy in the joy of knowing Jesus Christ. You are not going to have a happy church unless the people of the church are happy in their faith, happy in their love, happy in the joy of knowing Jesus Christ as Lord and Savior. People who know Jesus Christ are happy to forgive even when it's tough to forgive. They are happy to love, even though love is looked upon by both old and young in this world of ours as a kind of weakness. They are happy to help, because they have received from God Himself the help of all help: atonement through our Lord Jesus Christ.